# CHOOSING TO LIVE, CHOOSING TO DIE

## The Complexities of Assisted Dying

## NIKKI TATE

### Illustrations by
### BELLE WUTHRICH

ORCA BOOK PUBLISHERS

**Library and Archives Canada Cataloguing in Publication**

Title: Choosing to live, choosing to die: the complexities of assisted dying / Nikki Tate; illustrations by Belle Wuthrich.
Names: Tate, Nikki, 1962– author. | Wuthrich, Belle, 1989– illustrator.

Description: Series statement: Orca issues | Includes bibliographical references and index.

Identifiers: Canadiana (print) 20190069856 | Canadiana (ebook) 20190069864
| ISBN 9781459818897 (hardcover) | ISBN 9781459818903 (PDF) | ISBN 9781459818910 (EPUB)

Subjects: LCSH: Right to die—Juvenile literature. | LCSH: Euthanasia—Juvenile literature. | LCSH: Assisted suicide—Juvenile literature. | LCSH: Medical ethics—Juvenile literature.

Classification: LCC R726.T37 2019 | DDC j179.7—dc23

Library of Congress Control Number: 2019934028
Simultaneously published in Canada and the United States in 2019

**Summary:** This nonfiction book for teens examines the complex issue of medical assistance in dying from multiple perspectives. Illustrated with photographs.

*Orca Book Publishers is committed to reducing the consumption of nonrenewable resources in the making of our books. We make every effort to use materials that support a sustainable future.*

Orca Book Publishers gratefully acknowledges the support for its publishing programs provided by the following agencies: the Government of Canada, the Canada Council for the Arts and the Province of British Columbia through the BC Arts Council and the Book Publishing Tax Credit.

Edited by Sarah N. Harvey
Design by Belle Wuthrich
Cover and interior illustrations by Belle Wuthrich

ORCA BOOK PUBLISHERS
orcabook.com

Printed and bound in China.

22  21  20  19  •  4  3  2  1

For Helga—I wish I'd done better.
—NT

*Nikki's German grandparents on a visit to Banff, AB, with Nikki and her younger brother, Peter.*

# Contents

"Physician-assisted suicide and euthanasia have been profound ethical issues confronting doctors since the birth of Western medicine, more than 2,000 years ago."

—*Ezekiel Emanuel*

Oncologist and bioethicist

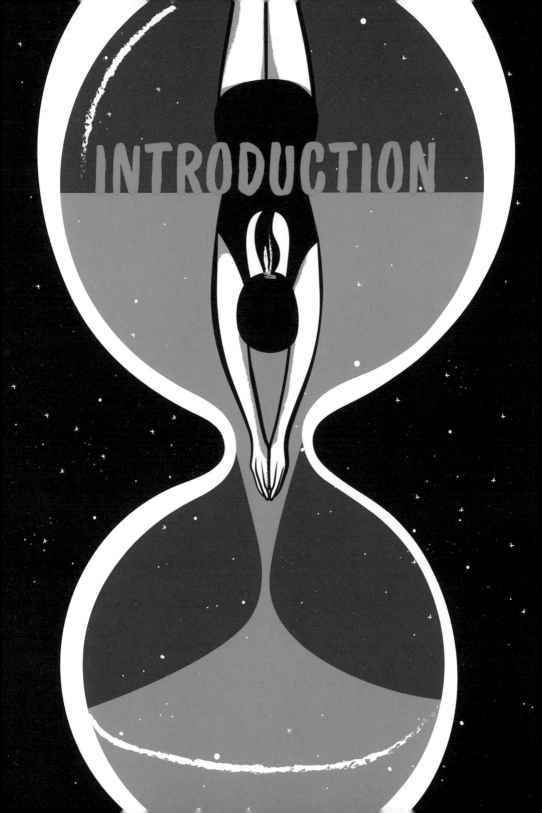

I walked for many hours on the trails near my home in the mountains while I grappled with complex questions that arose during the time I worked on this book.

**T**HIS BOOK IS ONE OF THE most challenging writing projects I've ever undertaken. Complex and multi faceted, the subject matter is both interesting to consider from an intellectual perspective and emotionally gripping. Grappling with difficult, sometimes contradictory ideas, I have tried to present the topic of **assisted dying** from a critical thinking perspective. To me this means being as fair-minded as possible when considering the main question: Is **medical assistance in dying** (sometimes referred to as MAID) an appropriate option for those nearing the end of life? I've tried to take into account my own biases, present ideas very different from my own, and better understand how we find ourselves where we are as a society. I've asked a lot of questions—and kept asking questions, because every

*Is medical assistance in dying an appropriate option for those nearing the end of life?*

time I found some clarity, some new piece of information would come to light and lead me to reconsider.

Because my research took me back and forth through books and scholarly articles, magazine opinion pieces and blog posts, documentaries and legal documents, as well as back in time through my own personal experiences, my understanding of the topic kept changing. You'll notice that the book's structure somewhat reflects that winding path through this complex topic. As with an intricately woven tapestry, pull on a thread in the religion section and something wiggles over in the ethics chapter. When I considered the comments of a medical doctor, the light fell differently on my memories of my grandmother. It was impossible to organize the material in a strictly chronological or thematic way, because all of the dimensions of this subject impact and relate to all of the others. Be patient as you read. We will loop back and forth through time and revisit topics in more depth or within a slightly different context as we go on our journey.

I've tried hard to cover the subject in such a way that murky areas would become clearer, but I ended up with almost as many questions as when I started. In truth, I added a few new ones I'd never considered. I hope you are able to bring this same spirit of open-mindedness and investigation to your reading of the material. And remember that life and death are rarely as straightforward as we'd wish.

Each year, many people visit Jim Morrison's grave in Paris, France.

## — DEATH COMES TO EVERYONE —

**NO ONE HERE GETS OUT ALIVE** is the title of a book about singer Jim Morrison of The Doors, but it's also a statement of fact. There are few things that every human being will experience. We may or may not be lucky enough to grow up in a loving family able to provide for our basic needs of food, clean water, shelter and education. We may experience war or natural disaster or we might avoid both. We may marry or remain single. We may have children or not. We may be sick or healthy, weak or strong, outgoing or introverted. We may be students, go to work each day or not work at all. We may live in a big city, on a tiny remote island or in a village in the mountains. The possibilities are endless. No matter where our lives take us, there is one thing that will happen to all of us: death.

What is not quite so clear is who and what determines when and how we die. Not so long ago, people died as a result of accidents, infections or sudden traumatic events like heart attacks or strokes. Many died from cancer because treatment did not exist, and many lives were lost to starvation. Though in some parts of the world starvation is still an awful reality, for the first time in human history more people on the planet are overweight than are underweight.

Advances in medicine and technology mean many people now survive previously life-ending illnesses. Now that we *can* extend life, the question is *should* we? If so, for how long? In our high-tech world of ventilators and feeding tubes, at what point should we let a body die? Who chooses the time, place and method of death? Who makes the final decision for someone who is desperately ill? God? Doctors? The patient? Family members? Mother Nature? Ask ten people and you will get ten different answers.

Caring conversations with family and friends
can help make end-of-life decisions easier.

## — WHAT DOES IT MEAN TO BE ALIVE? —

**IT'S USUALLY EASY TO ANSWER THIS** question when someone is healthy and enjoying life. But what about someone in a deep **coma** whose heart and lungs function only because of machines? What about someone with advanced **dementia** who no longer recognizes loved ones? What about a cancer patient who has tried all available treatments and now suffers endless pain? What choices are available to someone who no longer wonders *whether* their **terminal illness** will win but rather *how long* it will take? These individuals are all still alive—their hearts are beating and some may still be fully aware of their situations and able to eat, drink and get around on their own. But what if they, their families or their doctors decide their lives are not worth living anymore? Should these patients be allowed to have medical assistance in dying? Should humans be allowed to relieve suffering at the end of life, much as we do when we **euthanize** a beloved pet at the vet's office? Or is human life sacred and to be protected and extended no matter what? There are no easy or right answers to these questions. In the following chapters we'll look at the issue of medical assistance in dying (see other terms for this on pages 52–53) from various perspectives.

One day you, too, will die. In fact, everyone you know will die. Pretending it won't happen won't help you or those you love make the best decisions when the end of life approaches. Maybe you have experienced the death of a loved one and you have questions about how it all happened. As you read, consider what you think and feel about this issue. Have conversations with other people and listen with an open mind and a kind heart to their opinions. Not everyone will agree with you, and that's okay. Dying may be a universal experience, but it's also a deeply personal matter; each death is as unique as the person's life that came before.

Yes, it can be hard to think clearly about dying. Though it can be difficult to sort through the different perspectives, I believe that the more information that's made available about end-of-life options, the more we are able to make informed decisions, even under difficult circumstances.

"A right to live does not include an obligation to do so, under any or every circumstance. It is surely true that we can waive such a right, and this is the basis of our autonomy in end-of-life decisions."

—Dr. Rodney Syme

Author of *A Good Death: An Argument for Voluntary Euthanasia*

> ## "I want to die as well as my cat did a few years ago."
>
> —*Allan Scott*
> *Victoria Times Colonist,* October 2014

**F**EW OF US QUESTION WHETHER IT'S right to euthanize an animal that is suffering. It is much harder to make that decision when it comes to a person's life.

At the heart of the debate over whether medical assistance in dying should be easily available is the debate over whether it's more important to protect life at all costs or to provide each individual with the right to choose what is best for them.

## — MY STORY —

WHEN SURGEONS OPENED UP MY GRANDMOTHER'S belly to take out what they thought was a tumor in her liver, they discovered the cancer had spread to her stomach, spleen and kidneys. Without removing any tissue, they sewed her back up and sent her home to die. My grandmother was in the final stages of terminal liver cancer. Medicine could not cure her. For a few months it was possible to manage her pain and keep her comfortable by giving her large doses of **morphine**. But at the very end, even that was not enough.

My grandmother pleaded with my mother. "Please. Let me die. I have had enough."

Though assisted suicide is not legal in many places, the fact is that medical professionals, families and individuals make life-and-death decisions every day. In the case of my grandmother, when she was readmitted to the hospital just days before she died, she used the last of her strength to push away the nurses who were trying to give her food and water. "Make them stop," she begged. The nurses insisted on providing fluids through an *IV drip.* My grandmother tried to pull it out. Her doctor then had a conversation with my parents. I was not there (I was only thir-

As children, Nikki and her brother enjoyed visits to Germany to see their grandparents.

teen when all this was going on), but I was later told that the doctor offered to give my grandmother a mix of drugs that would combine a large dose of morphine with other medications that would ease her pain, send her into a deep sleep and speed the end her life.

My grandmother's mind was muddled from pain and the morphine she was already taking. She was no longer able to make the decision to end her life herself. Based on her actions (refusing food and water, asking that the nurses stop trying to treat her), my

## What Is a Brompton's Cocktail?

**B**ROMPTON'S COCKTAILS FIRST CAME INTO WIDE use in the 1920s and '30s. This mix of morphine, cocaine, alcohol, flavored syrup and a *sedative* called chlorpromazine eased pain for patients who were in the final stages of a terminal illness. A *stimulant* like cocaine was added to the mixture so patients could be functional enough to spend some time with their loved ones before dying. The official reason for providing such a potent mixture was to make the dying patient comfortable. A large enough dose of any sedative will hasten death. It was widely accepted (and still is) that speeding a patient's death may be a side effect of properly managing extreme pain at the end of life.

parents and the doctor concluded she was ready to die. At bedtime one evening, she was given a large dose of something similar to a Brompton's Cocktail, and she died quietly during the night.

Was that the right thing to do? She would have died anyway. But my family believes she suffered a little less during her final hours by being helped along.

Many years later, my mother was diagnosed with a different type of terminal illness. She was only in her fifties when she became very ill with a rare kind of dementia. Even though I knew she would have wanted to end her suffering sooner rather than later, by the time my mother's illness became very serious she was unable to

Nikki's mother, Helga, spending Christmas with family after being diagnosed with Pick's disease, a rare type of dementia.

express her thoughts. I had the chance to give her the equivalent of a Brompton's Cocktail when I was caring for her at home. But in the end, I chose not to. Not a day goes by that I don't ask myself whether I did the right thing.

## — THE THEORY AND PRACTICE OF DYING —

**MEDICAL ASSISTANCE IN DYING CAN TAKE** several forms. Some people believe it's important to give patients a painless, peaceful way to exit the world. Without this option, someone may turn to other methods of suicide that can be violent (and traumatic for those who discover the body). Some of these methods may not be completely reliable and may leave the person with irreversible injuries or brain damage that ultimately results in even more suffering. Worrying about these possibilities can cause terrible anxiety.

Protesters on both sides of the assisted-dying debate let
legislators know their positions.

In Oregon, where medical assistance in dying has been legal
since 1997, nearly half of the people approved to take advantage of
this option wind up dying a natural death, without ever using the
lethal prescription they have on hand. Having the option of choosing
when to die, and being in control of the act, is often enough to keep
people from resorting to other, more drastic, measures.

It may seem obvious to let someone make up her own mind
about when she is ready to die. After my grandmother's surgery it
was clear she wasn't going to get better. When she begged to be
allowed to die, it seemed that helping end her suffering would be
a kind thing to do. But though the idea made sense in theory, it
wasn't actually that easy to help her.

*END-OF-LIFE FACT*

In 2017, 6,585 deaths in the Netherlands were reported to be assisted deaths, an increase of 8 percent over the total reported in 2016.

## – SO MANY QUESTIONS –

IN MY FAMILY WE HAVE ASKED ourselves many of the questions you will consider in this book. As you read, it might be helpful to think about these ideas and questions from several different points of view. For example, how would you behave if you were confronted with situations similar to those we'll talk about? Just as importantly, consider why other people might come to a different decision. And think about how lawmakers and political leaders must balance the needs of many different people to come up with policies and laws that will best serve society as a whole.

As well, consider whether it's possible to measure suffering. Who should decide how much suffering is too much? A medical specialist who hardly knows the patient? The patient's regular doctor who knows them well but may not have the latest information about the illness and treatment options? The patient? What if the patient is unable to communicate or is in a coma? Should a family member be able to make end-of-life decisions for someone they love?

## Not Dead Yet

**N**OT DEAD YET (NOTDEADYET.ORG) IS A national grassroots disability rights group in the United States that opposes assisted suicide and euthanasia. Members believe it's very dangerous to legalize assisted suicide. Doctors can make mistakes, and it's nearly impossible to accurately predict how long someone might live with any disease. Most regulations require that a doctor decide when a person qualifies for assisted suicide. Instead of making it easier to die, opponents of assisted dying advocate finding ways to make living more comfortable. They believe that equal access to health care for all, including those with disabilities, chronic conditions and terminal illnesses, should be a priority. Some argue that changing laws may lead to normalizing death by making it too easy for doctors to prescribe lethal doses of medication.

What if the patient might actually get better if they endure a painful or unpleasant course of treatment? Should they be forced to go through the treatment before they give up? What if an experimental treatment is an option? Should the sick person be required to give it a try in order to help others through medical research?

What if someone is having a really bad day and can't imagine suffering any longer, even though it's possible that they may experience better days in the future? Who should decide whether an illness is severe enough to justify granting a patient's suicide wish? If someone's condition is managed with assistance from caregivers, powerful drugs or surgeries, should the person living with these challenges be the one to decide whether their life is worth living? What do we mean when we talk about someone's quality of life?

What if the patient in question is a child? Some illnesses affect babies and young children. They may be incurable and can challenge the resources of even the strongest families. Should a parent be able to decide whether a child should live or die?

The issue of assisted dying is further complicated by religious views, social norms and legal issues. And, of course, when individuals and family members are in the middle of a crisis, they must face the question of whether assisted dying is the right choice. Watching a loved one die is a deeply emotional experience. We rarely make our best decisions when we are upset, and there are few decisions more upsetting than deciding whether and when the time is right to end a life.

Should a family member be able to make end-of-life decisions for someone they love?

"Just as when we come into the world, when we die we are afraid of the unknown. But the fear is something from within us that has nothing to do with reality. Dying is like being born: just a change."

—Isabel Allende

Author

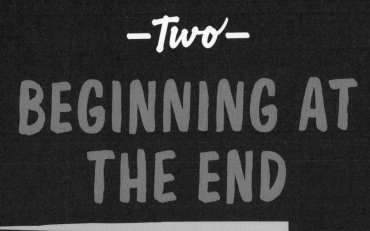

# —Two—
# BEGINNING AT THE END

**L**ONG BEFORE MY MOTHER BECAME ILL, she told me that if she ever developed Alzheimer's disease I should take her into the woods and shoot her. If I had actually shot my mother as she had asked, perhaps I could have argued that the act was an assisted suicide—even though I had pulled the trigger.

One of the arguments in favor of allowing assisted dying is to prevent exactly that sort of violent death by hanging, shooting, wrist-slitting and so on. Even under the umbrella of legally acceptable methods of assisted dying, there are several commonly understood options. So what do we mean, specifically, when we talk about *medically assisted death*?

## —FOUR OPTIONS—

1. **REMOVAL OF LIFE-SUSTAINING EQUIPMENT.** When someone in a coma (or *permanent vegetative state*) is declared to be brain-dead and unlikely to regain consciousness, the body can be kept alive by forcing oxygen into the lungs with a machine and providing nutrition through a feeding tube. When someone is speaking about a terminally ill and unconscious patient and they use the term "pulling the plug," it likely refers to removing the tube that supplies

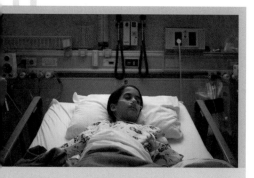

Modern medical equipment makes it possible to prolong life by supporting basic biological functions such as breathing.

oxygen to the patient. Unconscious people may be able to breathe on their own, but they will need to receive nutrition through a feeding tube. Removing a feeding tube, if this is the sole source of nutrition, will also result in a patient's death. It may take days or even weeks for a patient to die after a feeding tube is removed, depending on how weak or ill they are.

## Case Study: Terri Schiavo

**T**ERRI SCHIAVO WAS IN HER mid-twenties when she had a heart attack. Though she was revived, she had suffered major brain damage and wound up in a coma. For the next several years, efforts were made to rehabilitate her, but without any positive results. When it seemed that Terri would never recover but would remain in a permanent vegetative state, her husband asked to have her feeding tube removed. A long legal battle between Terri's parents and her husband followed. Terri's parents felt that because she was a Roman Catholic she would not agree with removing the feeding tube. Her husband argued that there was no chance of recovery and that Terri would not have wanted to be kept alive in this way. After fifteen years and many court battles, Terri's feeding tube was removed. She died thirteen days later.

2. **VOLUNTARY CESSATION OF EATING AND DRINKING.**
Sometimes a patient refuses to eat or drink as a way of hastening death. This method may be supported by comfort measures that include providing pain medication or sedation so the patient does not suffer from the effects of starvation.

## Case Study: Virginia Eddy

IN 1994 DR. DAVID EDDY WROTE an account of his mother's death in the *Journal of the American Medical Association*. He described how eighty-four-year-old Virginia Eddy had been very independent and happy until a series of medical conditions made it impossible for her to live alone. Though she was not suffering from a terminal illness as such, her quality of life was greatly diminished, and she felt ready to die.

"I know they can keep me alive a long time," she said, "...but what's the point? If the pleasure is gone and the direction is steadily down, why should I have to draw it out until I'm 'rescued' by cancer, a heart attack, or a stroke?"

Virginia and her son talked at length about treatment options for her various ailments, as well as methods she could consider for ending her life. "Is the meaning of life defined by its duration? Or does life have a purpose so large that it doesn't have to be prolonged at any cost to preserve its meaning?" she asked. "I don't want to spoil the wonder of my life by dragging it out in years of decay."

When Virginia somehow survived a bout of pneumonia, she decided to stop eating and drinking. On her eighty-fifth birthday she enjoyed a party with her family, and after eating a last piece of chocolate, she stopped eating and drinking. Six days later she died quietly while sleeping.

Dr. Rodney Syme believes some suicides can be prevented by providing people with choices and a sense of control as they reach the end of life.

3. **PHYSICIAN-ASSISTED SUICIDE.** In some places, physicians may prescribe a lethal dose of medication for a patient. The patient must be able to swallow the medication on their own; the doctor can prescribe lethal drugs but can't administer them. Over the past thirty years or so, Dr. Rodney Syme has counseled hundreds of patients nearing the end of life. He writes, "The provision of control over the end of life is the most powerful palliative for people approaching it ...The peace of mind and sense of security it provides are profound, and do not in any way dictate that medication that can be used to end life will be used for this purpose." Having access to lethal medication can, Dr. Syme observes, "actually prevent suicide."

4. **LETHAL INJECTIONS.** In a few places where medically assisted dying is legal, physicians are allowed to administer the lethal drugs. Lethal injections that combine two or three different drugs are used, and the doctor generally stays with the patient as the drugs take effect and until the patient is declared dead.

# WHY NOW?
## How Do People Decide When the Time Is Right?

**WHY DO PEOPLE SOMETIMES CHOOSE TO** end their lives early? Some of the most commonly mentioned reasons for wanting to have medical assistance in dying are listed below.

1.  **FEAR OF BEING A BURDEN ON OTHER PEOPLE.** When people are very ill, it can become difficult or impossible for them to complete even the most basic tasks. Many people don't want their loved ones to have to be responsible for doing everything from feeding and bathing them to turning them over in bed and providing medications or treatments. Some feel that allowing caregivers to be released from their responsibilities is a gift of love.

2.  **LOSS OF INDEPENDENCE.** For many, the idea of no longer being independent or able to make their own decisions is related to a desire to be able to make decisions about when and how they die.

**AVOIDANCE OF EXTREME PAIN.** Many people express a desire to avoid pain at the end of life. Other physical symptoms, like being unable to control bowel and bladder function, are also mentioned as reasons why a patient would consider medical assistance in dying.

**DESPAIR.** A loss of hope for the future is often linked with depression, and both are associated with an increased likelihood that the patient will be interested in medically assisted dying.

**FEAR AND UNCERTAINTY.** Fear of the future and uncertainty about what happens after death are also mentioned by patients who are facing end-of-life decisions.

**ANXIETY.** Many patients experience anxiety when they are no longer able to make important decisions for themselves, particularly when they are facing imminent death. Just knowing they can decide when to say "enough is enough" can reduce anxiety for many. By the same token, when patients know they have access to adequate pain management and, when the time comes, *palliative sedation*, they may feel reassured enough that death will not be an ordeal that they do not feel the need to ask for more aggressive intervention.

## END-OF-LIFE FACT

Some studies suggest that one in four cancer patients die without having their pain fully controlled.

# — WHERE DO WE DIE? —

**IT WASN'T THAT LONG AGO THAT** elderly family members were cared for at home, which is also where they died, usually without much medical intervention. After all, there wasn't much that medicine could do to prolong life. Over the past hundred years or so, it has become more and more likely for patients to spend their final days in some sort of institution. In North America, care homes (also known as nursing homes) became more common after World War II, as families became smaller and it was no longer as common for multiple generations to live together. Houses also became smaller, and women were more likely to have careers. Because they were working outside the home, women were often unable to stay home and care for elderly family members.

**PALLIATIVE CARE VISITOR ENTRANCE**

Although some care homes do have full medical facilities, most are only appropriate for people who can live quite independently or with some basic assistance with certain tasks. When patients are too ill to be cared for in a care home, they are often moved into a hospital setting. In a 2018 study conducted in Ontario, most people said they would like to die at home.

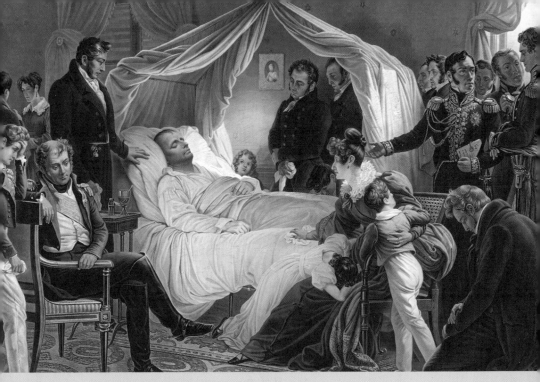

In the past, gathering at the deathbed typically occurred at home. Today people are much more likely to die in a hospital or other institution.

The reality is that about 70 percent of people die in institutions (hospitals, care homes or palliative care facilities)—a trend found across North America, where we have been moving away from end-of-life care at home. Fewer doctors are willing to make house calls, and not all physicians want to provide palliative care. These shifts in the way health care is delivered, together with changes in our relationship to death and dying, mean it is increasingly likely that death will occur away from home.

For many, the idea of dying in the care of strangers in a public place is unappealing. Because medical assistance in dying is not supported in all public facilities, some elderly patients are forced into the position of having to end their lives earlier than they may

## Case Study: The Importance of Independence

**H**ELEN WAS EIGHTY YEARS OLD WHEN, because of failing eyesight, she feared she would not be able to continue living alone in her home. Helen was referred to Dr. Rodney Syme, as she didn't want to become a burden on her adult daughter. She also did not want to move into a care home. Instead she wanted the option of choosing when and how to end her life.

After a lengthy series of consultations spread over a number of months, Helen eventually took a lethal combination of medications, as prescribed by Dr. Syme. Because Australian law prevented him from participating directly in any way, Dr. Syme did not stay with Helen but left her to consume the medication alone.

"Helen taught me the importance of independence, the loss of which could create existential suffering," he writes in *Time to Die*.

truly need to in order to avoid a long, slow decline in an impersonal facility. When there is no legal option for medical assistance in dying, patients are forced to take pre-emptive action, because once they move into a facility there won't be anyone to provide assistance.

It's easier to consider the option of a medically assisted death when the circumstances are reasonably clear-cut. It's when we begin to consider some of the more complex situations in which people have found themselves making life-and-death decisions that things become less clear.

One of the challenges hospitals face is how to establish policy that balances the wishes of competent minors against the desires of their parents. Although laws are currently in place to protect those under the age of 18, some argue that as long as a terminally ill child is fully informed and understands the impact of their decision, they should have a say in their end-of-life options.

"If you saw a person drowning in a pond, but there was a sign prohibiting access to the pond, would you trespass to save the person?"

———

—Dr. Henry Morgentaler

Physician and pro-choice advocate

# —Three—
# CONSIDER THE CONTEXT

**D**EPENDING WHERE YOU LIVE, IT MAY or may not be legal to help someone die. Choosing to do so anyway reflects how much one values personal independence in medical decision-making. At the same time, agreeing to help someone die might go against a family's belief that all life is sacred and may also conflict with a doctor's ethical position that a physician should never harm a patient.

Let's have a look at the different contexts in which we consider choices related to dying.

## — THE LAW —

LAWS HELP CREATE A SET OF rules that all citizens are expected to live by. What is legal at any given place and time has a major influence on how people behave. In most places in the world there are laws that prevent someone from helping another person hasten the end of life. If the law does not allow any exceptional circumstances, then helping someone else die is considered to be **premeditated murder.** If a person ends his or her own life but with some help, then the helper has assisted with a suicide, an act that is also considered to be illegal in most places.

When attitudes in society change, laws must also change to reflect the desire of the majority of people. Changing existing laws (or creating new ones) can take time, so sometimes there is a period when existing laws are broken until the legal system catches up to accepted practices.

# — VALUES, MORALS AND ETHICS —

**WHEN WE NEED TO MAKE A** decision about what to do in a particular situation, we tend to consider, often without realizing it, both our values and our morals. Sometimes ethics also come into play. When a decision is straightforward, that's often because our ethics, morals and values all align. When our morals tell us one thing and our ethics guide us in a different direction, decision-making can be a drawn-out, painful struggle.

What exactly do we mean when we talk about values, morals and ethics? There is some overlap in these terms and, in fact, various definitions for each. Here's my take on the terms and how they relate to medically assisted death.

## VALUES

**WHAT THINGS DO YOU CONSIDER TO** be most important in life? A person's values include the things that mean the most to them, that are really important. Values may change over time and vary from person to person. For example, one person may value having a large, comfortable home, while another could put privacy at the top of the list of their most important things. Having lots of friends may be

Many factors are considered when making end-of-life decisions, including the nature of the illness, the age of the patient, the laws of the land, religious beliefs and the norms of broader society.

very important to an elderly woman whose children and grandchildren live far away. She might spend a lot of time each week maintaining those friendships as a result.

One of the interesting things about values is that any particular value isn't really good or bad. Take the case of a social circle. For an artist who needs many hours a day of solitude to work on a painting, having too many people around might be disruptive. For an elderly woman, lots of people in a social group might be exactly enough to keep her engaged and enjoying her community.

When it comes to discussing end-of-life decisions, most people place a high value on being alive. Each of us, though, has our own idea of what a good quality of life involves, and often those distinctions have to do with our unique set of values, or what we feel to be most important. If an elderly man places a high value on being able to live alone in his apartment, he may resist making the choice to move into a care home. On the other hand, a man who has several close friends already living in the same care home may look forward to moving there. The care home may be the same, but the two men have different values and therefore have different reactions to giving up their apartments.

## MORALS

**MORALS TEND TO DIVIDE THE WORLD** into good and bad, black and white. Morals are shared among a group of people, often based on where someone lives and a common cultural or religious affiliation. Morals are usually fairly stable and don't change a lot over time. A culture or society tends to function smoothly if there is widespread acceptance of shared morals.

Most people agree that kindness is good; this is an example of a moral that is widely accepted. As a result, most people try not to be cruel. Cultures around the world consider it to be immoral to kill someone else. This is why it has been very difficult to come to an agreement about whether (and when) there may be exceptions to this nearly universal moral position. In other words, when is it kind to kill?

## ETHICS

**ETHICS ARE MORALS PUT INTO ACTION.** Most professions provide a clear set of ethical guidelines that relate to how their members should behave based on a shared set of moral assumptions. For example, lawyers and therapists must keep information about their clients confidential. A moral person (someone who has a strong sense of what is right and what is wrong) may or may not be brave or strong enough to act on his morals if the action is a difficult one. In the case of medical assistance in dying, the role of physicians is to care for patients and to extend life. However, doctors are also given the responsibility of relieving pain and suffering. There has long been a struggle between these two conflicting expectations.

What happens if medical assistance in dying is the only way to relieve pain and suffering when a terminally ill patient asks for help in speeding the arrival of the end? A physician will take into account their own values, the patient's values, the ethical guidelines of their particular hospital or clinic, and the laws of the place where they practice.

"Suffering is only intolerable when nobody cares. One continually sees that faith in God and his care is made infinitely easier by faith in someone who has shown kindness and sympathy."

—Dame Cicely Saunders
Doctor, writer and early advocate of the hospice movement

## END-OF-LIFE FACT

In 2016, almost half the deaths recorded in England took place in a hospital. Almost 6 percent of deaths occurred in a designated hospice facility.

# – PALLIATIVE CARE –

**THERE IS WIDESPREAD RELUCTANCE TO MAKE** it too easy to access medical assistance in dying, but there are alternatives that focus on keeping a dying patient comfortable without hastening death. *Palliative care* is one of the most commonly implemented end-of-life options.

According to the World Health Organization (WHO), palliative care aims to support a patient's end-of-life experience by providing pain relief as well as recognizing the need for psychological and spiritual care. Palliative care involves a team of helpers (volunteers and professionals) who assist not only the patient but also the patient's family members and loved ones as death approaches.

Palliative care providers accept that death is a natural part of life and don't try to hasten or delay death. Instead, according to the WHO website, they find ways to "help patients live as actively as possible until death."

The intended goals of palliative care make a lot of sense and have plenty of support within the medical community. Palliative care workers don't always see eye to eye with those in the medical field who support the option of medically assisted death. The reasons for this disagreement can be traced back to the origins of palliative and hospice care.

Dame Cicely Saunders, a doctor, founded the first modern **hospice** in England in 1967. She recognized the unique needs of dying patients and their loved ones. One of her convictions was that dying patients deserved to have their pain adequately controlled. Coming from a Catholic background, she blended her religious convictions with her medical knowledge and built the first facility in the United Kingdom (Saint Christopher's, in London) exclusively intended for implementing palliative care procedures.

Dame Cicely Saunders was an energetic and tireless advocate of providing care and comfort to patients nearing the end of life.

For some professionals who work with dying patients, accepting a patient's request for medical assistance in dying (MAiD) goes against the founding principles of Dame Saunders's original palliative care model. Palliative care workers have sometimes been very resistant to the idea of MAiD as an alternative to pain and comfort care at the end of life. The result has been open animosity between professionals who have aligned themselves on either side of the MAiD debate but who are all involved in caring for dying patients.

## Palliative versus Hospice Care

**D**EFINITIONS FOR PALLIATIVE AND HOSPICE CARE vary depending on where you live. In the United Kingdom, the terms are virtually interchangeable. In the United States, though, there are some differences.

* **Palliative care:** Usually provided in *acute care* hospitals. A team of professionals helps provide comprehensive care for dying patients.

* **Hospice care:** Though the services offered are similar in many respects, more than 80 percent of hospice care is provided in patients' homes. Most of the remainder of dying patients in hospice programs are cared for in long-term care facilities or designated hospices.

However, thinking is shifting, with a growing understanding that palliative care and MAiD are not mutually exclusive. The two approaches can complement each other to ensure that patients have access to the widest possible range of options when trying to decide how to best manage the final stages of a terminal illness. Some palliative care workers feel that the aims of palliative care (that death be dignified and without suffering) are, in fact, quite compatible with MAiD. Dealing with spiritual, family and relationship issues and putting one's affairs in order, as well as pain management and counseling should *all* be part of both palliative care and MAiD.

Because different ways of thinking about the question "Is it ever right to help someone else die?" can lead us to different conclusions, it's important to consider all these dimensions before making a decision. There's no doubt about it: dying can be complicated!

"Words—so innocent and powerless as they are, as standing in a dictionary, how potent for good and evil they become in the hands of one who knows how to combine them."

—Nathaniel Hawthorne

Novelist

# -Four-
# THE LANGUAGE OF DYING

Death and dying elicit powerful emotions. The words we choose to speak about this time of transition can have a powerful impact on our reactions and decision-making processes.

## – WISE WORDS: WHAT ARE WE TALKING ABOUT, ANYWAY? –

**Y**OU MAY HAVE ALREADY NOTICED THAT I use different terms when referring to assisted dying. The words we choose have tremendous power to influence how we think and feel. It's important to understand how language changes over time and also to be clear and precise when we debate a subject like assisted dying. Let's have a look at some of the words we use when we talk about this issue.

One commonly used term is *assisted suicide* (or **physician-assisted suicide**). While the meaning of the word *assist* is reasonably clear ("to help"), *suicide* is a bit trickier. The Merriam-Webster online dictionary defines suicide as "the act or an instance of taking one's own life voluntarily and intentionally." In some countries, suicide is illegal and someone who survives an attempt may face prosecution. In India, for example, a person convicted of attempting suicide may face a prison term of up to one year. In other places, suicide is legal but it is against the law to help or encourage another person to end their life.

Going back to the dictionary, the term *assisted suicide* is defined as "suicide committed with someone else's help in order to end suffering from severe physical illness." Merriam-Webster's definition of the more specific term *physician-assisted suicide* refers to the person as a patient and states that the suicide is "facilitated by means (such as a drug prescription) or by information (such as an indication of a lethal dosage) provided by a physician aware of the patient's intent." In other words, the doctor may provide information and sometimes medication, but the patient takes the lethal drugs without direct help.

*Medically assisted suicide* is another term often used to describe a situation where a person is helped through medical means to speed death. Some people believe *suicide* should not be part of any term describing the process. Suggested alternatives include *medical assistance in dying* (MAiD), *medically assisted death*, **voluntary euthanasia**, *aid-in-dying* and *death with dignity*. I'll use various terms as we continue our discussion, but I wonder if we need a new word altogether, one that reflects the modern reality of contemporary medicine and the changes it has brought to the way we think about what it means to be alive and how and when we would prefer to die.

# — WHEN IS A SUICIDE NOT A SUICIDE? —

WHEN PEOPLE THINK OF SUICIDE, WHAT often come to mind are the brutal methods people use to end their lives. Shooting, hanging, or walking in front of a train are examples of violent ways to end a life. They are also all the result of a person taking action, doing something that causes them to die. What happens when someone does not take action per se, but chooses to stop eating and drinking? The end result is the same—death—but we tend not to think of the slower, more passive approach as being the same as a more direct method of suicide.

Though we often use the word *suicide* as a noun in English, to describe the act we often add the word *commit* (as in, *Frank committed suicide*). Because committing suicide is considered to be a crime in some countries and has only relatively recently been decriminalized elsewhere, using the term *commit* was consistent with the way we talk about other crimes. Today some people prefer to treat *suicide* as a verb. "She suicided" may sound less like a criminal act, but it does little to remove the term from its connection with mental illness and its associated stigma. Advocates in the mental health field believe we need to speak openly about suicide but that we need to think carefully about the words we use. Some places use completely different language, particularly when it comes to describing someone who chooses to end life early when faced with a terminal illness. In the Netherlands, the phrase *termination of life on request* is used instead of *assisted suicide* or *euthanasia*.

*END-OF-LIFE FACT*

The World Federation of Right to Die Societies was founded in 1980 and is made up of fifty-one right-to-die organizations from twenty-six countries.

## — THE CHANGING MEANING OF EUTHANASIA —

THE WORD *EUTHANASIA* HAS HAD VARIOUS meanings over time. The original Greek word meant "a good death." Today *euthanasia* refers to a doctor either directly causing death or allowing death to occur without taking measures to prevent or delay it. In voluntary euthanasia, a patient requests that a doctor provide a lethal dose of medication. **Passive euthanasia** requires the doctor to either remove **life support** or withhold lifesaving treatment. This can happen when a patient is unable to request assistance in dying (for example, if the patient is **brain-dead**).

We sometimes think that words don't change, but in fact language is constantly evolving. New terms emerge (*smartphone*, *binge-watch* and *vape* are all new additions to the English language) and old ones fall out of favor (you don't hear the word *poppycock*, for example, being tossed into casual conversation too often). Sometimes a word stays the same but its meaning changes. That's the case with *euthanasia*.

As mentioned above, the ancient Greeks used the word to mean a good or easy death. Back then, there was no assumption that anyone helped a dying person along. Today, though, euthanasia is associated with the idea of a doctor "putting someone down," a phrase commonly accepted in the veterinarian's office as a synonym for putting a beloved pet "to sleep." How did we get from one meaning to the other?

In the 1700s, a Christian understanding of a good death meant that someone passed without pain between this world and the hereafter, the realm watched over by a benevolent God. At that time people believed that a pleasant death experience (more or less free of pain and panic) was a result of *divine intervention*; good Christians were blessed by God with the gift or reward of a smooth passing. Doctors cared for sick people, but when a person was considered to be beyond hope, the doctor left and care of the dying person was handed over to the family. Church representatives often helped ensure that the dying person was spiritually prepared to make the transition to God's realm.

By the middle of the nineteenth century, a good death was one that signified the triumphant end of a good life well lived. A good death was

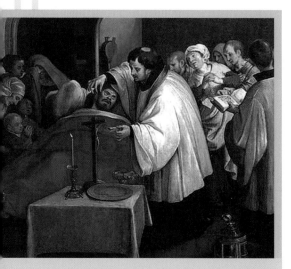

In the Catholic tradition, a priest may peform the last rites (prayers offered as a person nears death).

# Ars Moriendi

**T**HE EARLIEST HANDBOOKS FOR THE DYING were published in the 1400s. These religious texts provided instruction for both those who were dying and their families. Encouraging the dying to stay calm and not be afraid, and providing consolation that all would be well as long as one accepted Christ's salvation, was meant to help make death a peaceful experience. Instructions were also provided for family members who might find themselves looking after a dying person. Various other booklets with similar themes were produced over the next several hundred years.

Today euthanasia has come to mean the hastening of a patient's death by medical means.

no longer exclusively a religious experience, and doctors were often present at the deathbed. Though they couldn't change the course of events in terms of halting an inevitable death, doctors became more and more involved in helping patients remain comfortable during their final time alive. This new role of the doctor became associated with a new understanding of the term *euthanasia*. Today *euthanasia* has come to mean the hastening of a patient's death by medical means.

Sometimes the subjects of my art journal pages can be quite serious. Here, I'm struggling to find a personal connection with the often impersonal language of assisted dying.

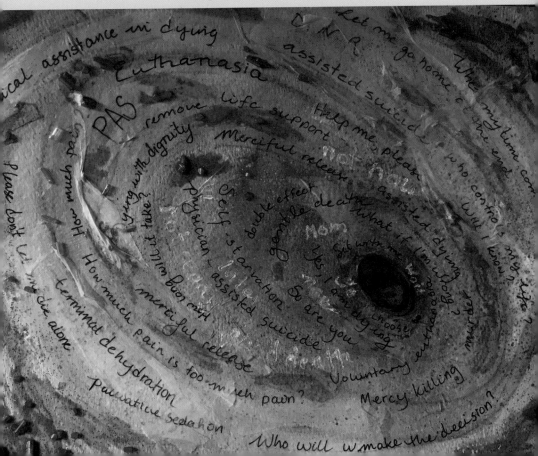

# FINDING THE RIGHT WORDS

THE FOLLOWING TERMS ALL RELATE TO some aspect of assisted dying. Though all of these terms refer to helping someone die, each has a slightly different connotation. Being precise about which words to use can help when discussing complicated issues like assisted dying. Keep in mind that these terms continue to evolve and may also vary from place to place.

* **AID-IN-DYING:** synonymous with physician-assisted suicide

* **DYING WITH DIGNITY:** a movement based on the philosophy that each person should be able to choose the time, place and manner of their own death

* **EUTHANASIA:** painlessly killing a patient who is suffering from a terminal illness

   **ACTIVE:** when a patient's life is ended by taking a direct action, like administering a lethal dose of medication

   **NON-VOLUNTARY:** when a physician carries out euthanasia without a patient's consent (e.g., in a case where the patient is in a coma)

   **PASSIVE:** withdrawal of medical treatment that is keeping a patient alive (e.g., removal of a feeding tube)

   **VOLUNTARY:** when a patient agrees to allow a physician to end their life

**GENTLE DEATH:** a term thought by some to be more appropriate than one including the word *suicide*

**MEDICAL ASSISTANCE IN DYING (MAiD):** when a physician provides direct assistance in killing a patient, usually through the administration of a lethal dose of medication (see also physician-assisted suicide)

**MERCIFUL RELEASE:** the end of something (in this context, a life) that seems fortunate because what preceded the end was painful or involved suffering

**MERCY KILLING:** synonymous with euthanasia

**PALLIATIVE SEDATION/TERMINAL SEDATION:** interchangeable terms referring to the practice of completely relieving a dying patient's pain and suffering by providing sedation so deep that the patient is rendered unconscious

**PHYSICIAN-ASSISTED SUICIDE:** when a patient ends their life with the help of a physician; help may take the form of a prescription, advice or both (see also MAiD)

**SELF-ADMINISTERED MEDICAL ASSISTANCE IN DYING:** when an eligible person takes lethal medication themselves in order to bring about death, and the medication is provided by a physician or nurse practitioner

**TERMINAL DEHYDRATION:** dehydration that results in death

# — EXTENDING LIFE OR DELAYING DEATH —

**IF DECIDING ON WHAT TERM TO** use is complicated, things get even trickier when we think about the hidden messages of language in the context of a conversation. What is the difference between a doctor saying, "If we provide a feeding tube, we can extend your grandmother's life" and "If we provide a feeding tube, we are delaying her death." The first sentence makes it seem like inserting the feeding tube when Grandma is no longer able to eat is a heroic measure that will keep her with us for as long as possible. Surely that's a good thing, right? But what if eighty-seven-year-old Grandma is in a lot of pain, has already outlived her beloved husband by several years and has expressed a desire to die? The second sentence sounds like we are forcing nutrients into a body that is trying to die, perhaps causing poor Grandma to suffer needlessly. When a family and a patient are trying to decide how much medical intervention is appropriate at the end of life, how a doctor phrases questions like this can be very important.

Seattle-based cardiologist Dr. Thomas Preston writes about the language we use to describe choosing not to take an action that would save a life. When patients have a **Do Not Resuscitate (DNR) order** on file, they are asking that no drastic measures (e.g., **cardiopulmonary resuscitation**, or CPR) be taken in a medical emergency. By *not* acting, medical personnel are in fact "killing" the patient. The word *kill* has negative connotations. Instead, Dr. Preston observes, if we use a phrase like *allowing the patient to die naturally*, the physician is no longer seen to be causing the patient's death.

Dr. Preston points out that there is a similar distinction to be made when life-sustaining treatment is withdrawn (as when a patient is taken off a ventilator). "Regardless of intent or propriety," he says, "the act deprives a person of life, and so constitutes killing, but not murder."

When you are reading arguments on either side of the debate, keep in mind that the author will likely be using the words and language most likely to sway your opinion. It's hard to find words that are truly neutral when the subject matter is so controversial.

Dr. Thomas Preston holds a copy of the first annual report on Washington State's *Death With Dignity Act in* 2010.

"The active participation
by one individual in
the death of another
is intrinsically
morally and
legally wrong."

—The Honourable
John Sopinka

Supreme Court of Canada judge

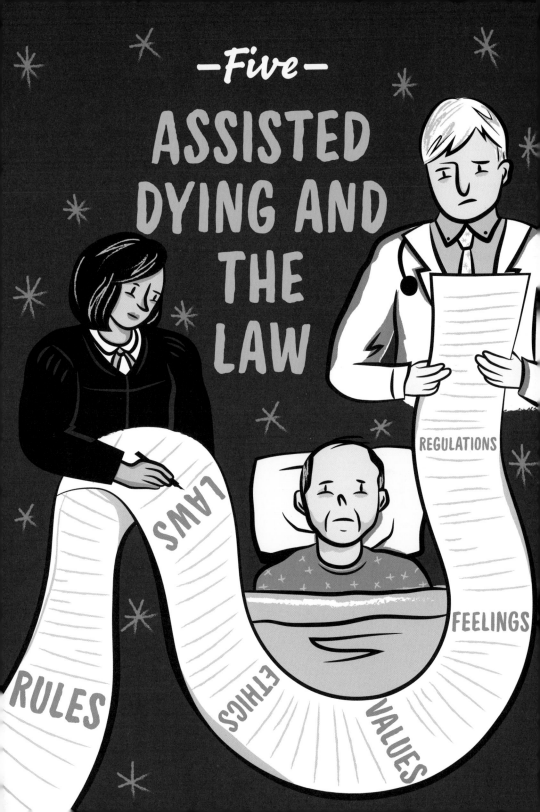

Courts of law are constantly reassessing what is considered right or wrong and legal or illegal.

## — IS KILLING SOMEONE ACCEPTABLE OR NOT? —

**I**N THE NEXT FEW CHAPTERS WE'LL take a closer look at the arguments for and against assisted dying. Let's first look at the issue by considering how legal thinking about assisted dying has changed over the years—and continues to change.

In the past, killing someone (unless in the context of war, a complicated subject for another book) was considered to be murder (or *manslaughter*) regardless of the circumstances. In many places today, this is still the case.

# — WHERE IS MAiD LEGAL? —

(AS OF APRIL 2019)

**SWITZERLAND WAS ONE OF THE FIRST** countries to consider a legally approved means of helping terminally ill people choose when they died. Since 1941 it has been legal there to assist someone for medical reasons, though ***active euthanasia*** has never been permitted. There isn't actually specific legislation in Switzerland that allows a patient to access medical assistance in dying. Instead, it's the fact that the act of helping someone commit suicide for unselfish reasons is *not* specifically mentioned in the criminal code that makes it not illegal to assist a dying person.

There are Swiss laws, however, that prohibit people from taking an active role in euthanasia and that forbid assistance with a suicide for selfish reasons (for example, if the helper is going to receive a large inheritance). As social acceptance has spread elsewhere in the world, the Swiss position has made the country a destination for patients unable to access such help in their home country.

# — LEGAL ARGUMENTS —

**ONE OF THE ARGUMENTS IN FAVOR** of legalizing physician-assisted dying is that if it were legal, the activity would no longer be conducted in secret. When assisted dying occurs in the open, it's easier to create formal regulations, make sure rules are followed and monitor the procedure. Those in favor of changing laws and implementing guidelines suggest that this should make the process safer and less subject to abuse.

But how does the law differentiate between causing a death for selfish or malicious reasons and causing a death to prevent the suffering of someone who is very ill? How can a law that allows people to take control of end-of-life decisions also protect the most vulnerable members of society?

Cardinal Bernard Law, the Archbishop of Boston, makes a good point when he asks, "Is serious illness a good enough reason to have a specific exception to the law?"

If the protection of life is one of the fundamental cornerstones of civilization, then changes in the laws that make it easier to die (and help someone else die) must be examined very carefully. It is estimated that only a tiny percentage of deaths actually qualify to be considered for assisted dying. It is also legitimate to ask whether it makes sense to change a law when it will apply to relatively few people.

The Vermont Alliance of Ethical Healthcare asked whether it was worth legalizing assisted dying when doing so opens the door for so many risks, including possible abuse by someone who may benefit from the early death of another person. Though many in Vermont shared concerns like these, the Patient Choice at End of Life Act took effect in the state on July 1, 2016.

Statistics collected so far in places like Oregon and the Netherlands seem to indicate that adequate protections are in place to prevent anyone from taking advantage of the new laws.

In 2016 protesters in Ottawa rallied against Bill C-14, the legislation that made it legal to access MAiD.

## – MURDER VERSUS SUICIDE? –

**HOW CAN YOU ACTUALLY TELL THE** difference between a murder and an assisted suicide? It would be very difficult to prove in a court of law that someone was killed in an act of assisted suicide when, in fact, they may have been murdered. The person may have been terminally ill in both cases, but if the motivation of a family member was, for example, to have quicker access to an inheritance, then the death would be considered a murder. But how could this be proved in court?

When laws change to allow medically assisted death, the many restrictions and regulations may seem overzealous, but the intent is to build in safeguards that prevent abuse of the law. This is why it's so important for courts and political leaders to remain vigilant and take their time when considering legal changes that have such potentially serious consequences.

In the past, the harsh Arctic environment meant the death of an elderly person was occasionally hastened for the sake of preserving scarce resources for other community members.

## — WHERE IS MEDICAL ASSISTANCE IN DYING LEGAL? —

**THE OFFICIAL DECISION TO ALLOW MEDICAL** assistance in dying is not made quickly or lightly and takes many years to implement. In 2002 both the Netherlands and Belgium passed laws that allowed patients to access both assisted suicide and active euthanasia, though in the Netherlands assisted dying was quietly practiced as early as 1970 and unofficially allowed as early as 1984. In 2009 Luxembourg passed assisted suicide legislation, and in Canada a law allowing medical assistance in dying for terminally ill patients came into effect in 2016.

In Canada, though the existing law prohibiting assisted suicide was not overturned until 2015, it was inconsistently applied for many years before that. For example, in 1949 an Inuit man called Eerkiyoot helped his very sick mother to commit suicide. Though not a regular occurrence, it was not unheard of for the very old or very sick to commit suicide in order to help preserve limited resources in a harsh environment. Though Eerkiyoot's actions were illegal at the time, a jury found that his decision to help was understandable and made sense within the context of his community. Because his actions were still against the law, the judge and jury found Eerkiyoot guilty, but he received a very light sentence of one year and only served half that time in jail.

## When Is a Law Imperfect?

SOMETIMES THERE'S A GAP BETWEEN THE way a law is written and the way it works in the real world. This can happen when a law is widely seen to be unjust or imperfect and, as a result, is rarely enforced. Such laws can sometimes stay in effect for a long time when people believe that changing the law and trying to implement new regulations would be too difficult politically and might galvanize opposition. Sometimes it's believed to be better to leave an imperfect law in place and sort of ignore it. In states like Oklahoma and Michigan, where attempts to decriminalize assisted dying actually resulted in stricter regulations being put in place, some people believe it might have been better to leave the laws alone. Other legislation relating to abortion access and legalization of marijuana face the same challenge as societal norms and expectations change.

In the United States, legislation varies by state. Oregon was the first to implement a Death with Dignity law, in 1997, after voters chose to legalize physician-assisted suicide in a close vote (51 percent) in 1993. The law in Oregon allows physician-assisted suicide for patients residing in Oregon who are terminally ill and who have been told they have less than six months to live.

As of April 2019, Vermont, Hawaii, Washington, California, Colorado, New Jersey and Washington, DC, have implemented laws permitting assisted dying under certain circumstances. Other states have attempted to follow Oregon's lead, but in some cases (e.g., Maryland, Iowa, Oklahoma, Virginia) lawmakers confirmed or strengthened existing laws banning assisted dying. Courts in the United States continue to struggle to agree on whether people have a constitutional right to choose when and how they die.

## Case Study: Victor Hayes

VICTOR HAYES WAS AN ALCOHOLIC WHO had various medical ailments that he felt he could no longer live with. In 1985 he asked his girlfriend, Lois Wilson, to help him kill himself. The pair drove to Lake Ontario, where Victor asked Lois to push him off the end of the dock and into the water, knowing he could not swim. Eventually Lois did as she was asked. Lois had second thoughts and tried to pull him to safety but wasn't able to. Though she ran to get help, Victor Hayes drowned and Lois Wilson was convicted of aiding and abetting a suicide. She was sentenced to six months in prison, a much lighter sentence than the maximum of fourteen years.

In his excellent book *A Good Death: An Argument for Voluntary Euthanasia*, Dr. Rodney Syme describes his journey from being relatively clueless about how to help his dying patients to openly challenging laws banning voluntary euthanasia in Australia. Over the course of his career, Dr. Syme has counseled over 1,500 people about end-of-life options and provided lethal medication and instructions for using it to about 100. Despite publicly admitting he has played a role in assisting so many patients in choosing when and how to end their lives, to date Dr. Syme has not been prosecuted.

Laws against assisted dying remain in place in most countries, but it is not unusual for authorities to turn a blind eye to medical practices that may hasten death. For countries like the Netherlands and Canada that now have laws permitting some form of assisted dying, the path to changing the law was paved by doctors, activists and caring individuals determined to alleviate the suffering of the terminally ill. Though in many cases those who assisted with a suicide were not convicted, those found guilty usually did not serve much, if any, time in prison.

In Canada, even though medical assistance in dying has been decriminalized, the details of regulations are still being debated. Because of the way Canada's health-care system operates, even though the federal law changed, each province has some flexibility in terms of how the law is interpreted and how regulations are applied.

It is neither quick nor easy to change a law, particularly when the law is controversial. For some, waiting for the courts and lawmakers is simply not an option. Working quietly behind the scenes, some individuals (like Dr. Syme) choose to take matters into their own hands and act in a way that aligns with their values, beliefs and morals (though not necessarily with the law).

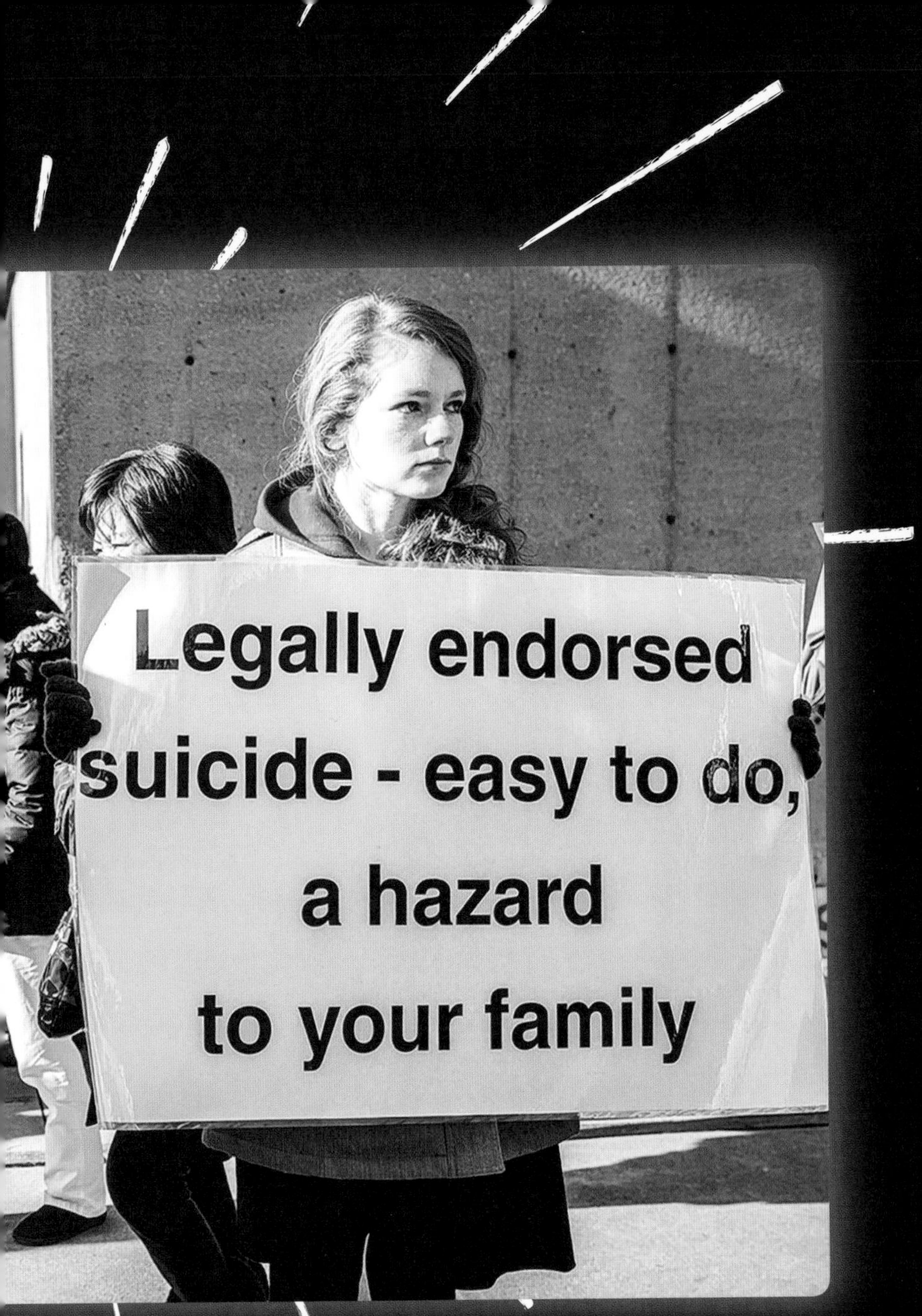
Legally endorsed
suicide - easy to do,
a hazard
to your family

# — DOCTOR DEATH —

**DR. JACK KEVORKIAN BECAME WELL** known in the early 1990s when he helped a fifty-four-year-old patient commit suicide. His "suicide machine" was loaded with three chemicals and then attached to his patient. When the patient pushed a lever, the chemicals were injected into an intravenous line and delivered into the patient's bloodstream. Not everyone agreed with Dr. Kevorkian's methods, and he was soon known by the nickname Doctor Death. Charged four times between 1994 and 1997 with assisting in a suicide, Dr. Kevorkian was acquitted three times. His fourth trial ended with a mistrial. In 1999 he was charged with second-degree murder after he injected a patient with a lethal dose of medication. Found guilty, Dr. Kevorkian spent eight years in jail before being released on parole in 2007. He died in 2011.

Not everyone agreed with Dr. Kevorkian's methods, and he was soon known by the nickname Doctor Death.

# Case Study: Who Owns My Life?

**A**MYOTROPHIC LATERAL SCLEROSIS (ALS) IS AN incurable degenerative disease that paralyzes those it affects. Though many patients die within five years, for some the disease can linger for many years, eventually taking away their ability to speak, swallow or breathe. When Sue Rodriguez was diagnosed with ALS in 1991, it was illegal in Canada to help someone commit suicide. But because she wanted to be able to end her life with a doctor's help, she challenged the law in British Columbia in 1992. She lost her case, but she appealed—and lost again. During her struggle she asked, "If I cannot give consent to my own death, whose body is this? Who owns my life?" These questions are central to the debate about assisted dying.

Believing that she should have the same right to commit suicide as someone who was not paralyzed, Sue Rodriguez challenged the lower court decision at the national level by appealing to the Supreme Court of Canada in 1993. In a close (5–4) decision, the Supreme Court upheld the existing law, stating that it was more important for the state to protect life at all costs than it was to allow people like Sue Rodriguez to have full control over decisions relating to their own bodies. The judges who argued for a new law felt the existing legislation discriminated against physically disabled persons, who would be breaking the law if they asked for help to commit an act that was legal for able-bodied individuals.

In February 1994, an anonymous doctor helped Sue Rodriguez die by giving her a lethal mixture of medications. A member of Canada's parliament, Svend Robinson, also attended her death as a witness and friend. Though the death was investigated, no charges were laid.

Dr. Philip Nitschke with a kit containing the equipment he used to assist patients who wished to die.

In Australia, assisted dying was legal for a short time in the Northern Territory. In 1996 Dr. Philip Nitschke became the first doctor in the world to legally inject a lethal dose of medication in a voluntary euthanasia. The law, known as the Rights of the Terminally Ill Act, came into effect in 1995 but was overturned by Australia's national government in 1997. During the time it was legal, four patients took advantage of having the right to choose when and how to die.

People like Sue Rodriguez and Lee Carter (a woman suffering from a serious disease affecting the spinal cord) were powerful voices speaking out on behalf of the right-to-die movement in Canada. The court case *Carter v. Canada* asked whether the law banning physician-assisted dying violated the constitutional rights of Canadians. In 2015 the Supreme Court of Canada decided that if someone is very ill and unable to end their life without help, it

## END-OF-LIFE FACT

A Supreme Court decision in 1997 stated that Americans do not have a constitutionally protected right to commit suicide.

is unconstitutional to deny them assistance from a physician. The court recognized that someone in this position must then either act prematurely (while still able) or suffer until death eventually arrives by natural causes. The court recognized that the choices available under the current law were cruel, that all citizens should have the right to choose suicide as an option, and that terminally ill patients should have the right to ask for medical assistance.

Laws relating to assisted dying are changing constantly, and by the time this book is published the legal landscape will have changed once again. For the first time in twenty-one years, an Australian state has passed legislation that will permit a terminally ill patient to get medical help to die. The law goes into effect in 2019, and critics say that the way the law is written is

Demonstrators at the Assembly of the Republic in Lisbon, Portugal, in May 2018 protest against euthanasia and ask for improved palliative care.

not perfect (applicants must meet sixty-eight criteria before being approved, a list that excludes some who should perhaps qualify).

In May 2018 in Guernsey (an island in the English Channel), members of the legislature voted against allowing assisted dying even though there is more and more support for this option among members of the general population.

While the law clearly shapes how people behave with regard to this subject, medicine, philosophy, finances and religion all shape our views as well. We'll consider these perspectives in the next few chapters.

"The easing of death, as an intentional double effect, is commonplace in palliative care and general practice."

———

−Dame Jessica Corner

**Professor of Nursing**

# — MEDICAL ISSUES —

THE *HIPPOCRATIC OATH* WAS WRITTEN ABOUT 2,000 years ago by the Greek physician Hippocrates (sometimes known as the Father of Medicine) and is often referred to as the ultimate set of principles by which physicians operate (no pun intended). Various translations exist and a few key phrases are well known and much discussed.

People often mention the phrase "First do no harm" as being central to a doctor's mandate. In fact, that exact phrase isn't included in the original version of the Hippocratic Oath, though Hippocrates did say a doctor should order a good diet for patients and be sure they suffer no hurt or damage. If we interpret this to mean that a doctor should do no harm, it's fair to ask whether keeping someone alive after they've indicated they no longer wish to live is, in fact, causing harm.

The Greek physician Hippocrates is sometimes called the Father of Medicine.

There is wording in the Hippocratic Oath that specifically prohibits giving someone poison, but historians believe this was more a reminder to physicians not to become involved in murder plots! Some scholars say it was not uncommon in ancient Greek city–states for doctors to ease a patient's suffering by providing medication.

Others point out that various other directives mentioned in the original oath have long since been abandoned. Originally, those taking the oath agreed not to perform surgery or charge for services. They also swore to Apollo (and various other gods and goddesses) that they would honor the promises they made.

The oath has been revised and adapted over the centuries. According to one article, a 1993 survey of 150 US and Canadian medical schools revealed that "only 14 percent of modern oaths prohibit euthanasia."

I suspect it is easier for both institutions and individual physicians to quote easy-to-understand directives like "do no harm" and "administer no poisons" than it is to deal with the complex realities of modern medical practice. One doctor has said, "Hippocrates never had a patient on a ventilator."

This ancient piece of papyrus contains a very early copy of the Hippocratic Oath.

Though some claim the Hippocratic Oath specifically prohibits euthanasia, bioethicist Dr. Steven H. Miles says, "The Greek-derived word *euthanasia* (literally, good death) was not coined until 280 BCE, about a century after the Oath was written. This new word did not refer to assisting death; it referred to a natural death without agony."

*Modern medicine has changed the way we respond to illnesses and accidents once thought to be life-ending.*

In reality the practice of medicine has changed dramatically over the past century. Advances in emergency interventions have changed the way we live and the way we die. Some examples are:

1. **CARDIOPULMONARY RESUSCITATION (CPR),** which was not used prior to 1960

2. **SOPHISTICATED SURGICAL TECHNIQUES** (the first successful heart transplant in a human was done in 1967)

3. **ANTIBIOTICS** (before penicillin became widely available in the middle of the twentieth century, patients died because of infections that are now easily treatable)

4. **RECENT TREATMENTS** that have the potential to extend life, including stem cell therapy, targeted cancer therapies, lab-grown skin and a new class of antibiotics

**BECAUSE MEDICINE CAN SAVE LIVES AND** extend them in ways we could not have imagined a hundred years ago, people are routinely living longer. Today the average life expectancy in the United States is seventy-eight years. But while we are living longer, we are not necessarily living better; we often live longer while suffering from incurable illnesses. The RAND Corporation (a global policy think tank) estimates that 40 percent of deaths in the United States are preceded by a period of dementia and slow decline lasting up to ten years. These new realities mean we need to modify the way we think of medical intervention as the end of life approaches.

Doctors have played key roles in changing attitudes about when it may be appropriate to help a patient die. One of the first known references to a doctor's active partici- pation in a patient's death is described in a German medical publication from 1800. The doctor talks about the terrible suffering he witnessed when patients were dying of what he called consumption (most likely *tuberculosis*). In such cases, he believed it was morally acceptable to provide a dose of medication that ended the patient's life.

At about the same time, German doctor Christian Ludwig Mursinna admitted he had helped a cancer patient die. Though other doctors in Christian countries may have been hastening death in incurable patients, very few wrote publicly about their support for the practice.

In the early 1800s a few doctors, including Christian Ludwig Mursinna, admitted to helping terminally ill patients die.

In 1988 the *Journal of the American Medical Association* published an article by an anonymous young doctor who described providing a deadly dose of morphine to a terminally ill cancer patient. The article, "It's Over, Debbie," generated an immediate backlash from doctors horrified at the physician's brazen act based on only a quick examination of the patient. Other doctors supported the decision. The discussion generated by the article continues today, despite the fact that legislation allowing assisted dying under certain circumstances has been put in place in many American jurisdictions.

In 1991 Dr. Timothy Quill published an account of helping a leukemia patient die. The article generated many responses,

"I retreated with my thoughts to the nurses' station. The patient was tired and needed rest. I could not give her health, but I could give her rest."
—Anonymous

Dr. Timothy Quill was the plaintiff in an assisted-suicide case known as *Vacco v. Quill*. Here, Dr. Quill is outside the Supreme Court in Washington, DC, in January 1987.

including letters from other physicians who stated that helping someone commit suicide, no matter what the circumstances, is always morally wrong.

Though Dr. Quill was never charged in his patient's death, a group of doctors and terminally ill patients challenged New York's ban on assisted suicide. The case (known as *Vacco v. Quill*) was eventually heard by the United States Supreme Court. The final verdict was that assisted suicide was not, and should not, be legal. That said, the Supreme Court justices agreed that patients at the end of life had every right to receive medication and treatment to help ease pain and suffering—even when that same treatment might have the "side effect" of hastening death.

Dr. John Bodkin Adams was a controversial figure, accused of murdering many of his elderly patients.

## — THE DOUBLE EFFECT —

**IN MANY JURISDICTIONS WHERE MEDICALLY ASSISTED** dying is illegal, it still may be possible to provide aggressive pain management for patients, even when giving large doses of drugs like *opioids* (morphine, OxyContin, Vicodin and so on) may speed death. In England in 1957, Dr. John Bodkin Adams was charged with murder after providing large doses of heroin and morphine to an eighty-one-year-old stroke victim. Justice Devlin told the deliberating jury that "the giving of drugs to an elderly patient to alleviate pain was lawful even if incidentally it shortened the patient's life." The idea that medication used for one purpose (relieving pain) could also have other physical impacts (slowing breathing, speeding death) is known as the *double effect*. Dr. Adams was not convicted, though he was suspected of providing inappropriate treatment causing death in 163 cases. Whether Dr. Adams was a mercy killer or a mass murderer is still debated today.

According to Jessica Corner, director and deputy dean of nursing at the Centre for Cancer and Palliative Care studies at Royal Marsden Hospital in London, England, "the easing of death, as an intentional double effect, is commonplace in palliative care and general practice." Other terms used to describe the use of deep sedation and pain management include **pharmacological oblivion, management of terminal anguish** and **terminal sedation**.

It has been fairly common practice for many years to accept the fact that administering a large enough dose of one medication (like morphine) intended to control pain may also cause side effects like slowed breathing, central nervous system depression and even death. Though the side effects are unintended and not the primary purpose of administering the drug, when death results it is considered acceptable and not likely to be prosecuted under laws preventing assisted suicide or murder unless an ulterior motive is identified.

> *Though the side effects are unintended and not the primary purpose of administering the drug, when death results it is considered acceptable.*

# — ARE DOCTORS BETTER THAN THE REST OF US? —

**EVEN IF A PERSON IS PROVIDED** with all the necessary information and they are willing to make the decision to terminate their own life, it is possible that they won't be able to carry out the act themselves. In this case, who takes on the medical responsibility for terminating a life?

Doctors are often the ones who must make life-and-death decisions with, or on behalf of, their patients. Though most doctors are compassionate and act in ways that serve the best interests of their patients, they are only human. Physicians are vulnerable to political, personal and financial pressures and sometimes make decisions that are not the best for the patient. Critics of more liberal euthanasia laws fear that legalizing assisted death could make it easier for unscrupulous physicians to escape conviction when inappropriate medical practices lead to the deaths of patients.

## Exit International

**E**XIT INTERNATIONAL WAS FOUNDED IN 1997 by Dr. Philip Nitschke, a controversial and outspoken supporter of assisted dying. Dr. Nitschke says, "I believe it is a fundamental human right for every adult of sound mind to be able to plan for the end of their life in a way that is reliable, peaceful and at a time of their choosing." Exit International believes control over one's life and death to be a fundamental civil right from which no one of sound mind should be excluded. The organization provides information and support to those exploring options at the end of life.

# — DO DOCTORS HAVE THE RIGHT TO SAY NO? —

**LIKE ALL OF US, DOCTORS COME** from many different backgrounds and hold a wide range of religious beliefs. What happens when a doctor who is also a practicing Catholic works at a hospital where medically assisted dying is an established practice? Should doctors be forced to carry out a patient's wishes if that request is legal but goes against the doctor's religious beliefs? What about the opposite situation? Should a doctor be able to help a patient die if that patient happens to be in a hospital where policies do not permit assisted dying?

In Canada, where assisted dying has only recently become legal, questions like this are being hotly debated. In some communities, the main hospital may be run by a religious organization while receiving public funding from taxes paid by all citizens. Should a facility that operates using taxpayer funds be allowed to deny a citizen access to a legal service based on religious or philosophical convictions?

Doctors continue to play a critical role in how we think about medically assisted death. Though some are outspoken in their support for change, others, like Australian doctor Karen Hitchcock, argue that some patients already feel worthless and a burden. Dr. Hitchcock is concerned that providing patients with the option of euthanasia will make it too easy to agree that someone's life is not worth living.

In Canada, Dr. Ellen Wiebe is challenging aspects of the new Canadian law that allows medical assistance in dying but also

**I** **LIVE IN THE BOW VALLEY IN ALBERTA,** where two local hospitals have very different views of assisted dying. In Banff, where the hospital is run by Covenant Health, a Catholic health-care organization, a strict policy prevents assisted dying. Because the hospital was founded and continues to operate based on Catholic moral and social traditions, assisted dying is considered to be a form of abandonment of a patient at the end of life. Instead, great effort is made to provide not only excellent medical care at the end of life but also companionship and support for a person's spiritual needs as death approaches. If a patient insists on medical assistance in dying, they are transferred to Canmore General Hospital, twenty-five minutes away. In Canmore, protocols are in place that allow patients to access medical assistance in dying.

While this system may seem adequate, several questions arise. Should very ill patients be forced to move from one facility to another when they are at their most weak and vulnerable? If a doctor in Banff is willing to provide assistance, should the local hospital be allowed to prevent access to a patient in order to remain true to the institution's operating principles?

permits institutions to decide whether to allow the procedure to take place. When asked for a medically assisted death by an elderly patient living in an Orthodox Jewish nursing home, Dr. Wiebe's assessment indicated that the patient qualified for the procedure. After the doctor met with the patient and his family and eventually administered a lethal dose of medication, the nursing home registered a formal complaint against Dr. Wiebe with the

*Her priority was to honor the wishes of the patient.* ✳

British Columbia College of Physicians and Surgeons. The CEO of the facility, David Keselman, told the *Vancouver Sun* that it was inappropriate to "have a doctor sneak in and kill someone without telling anyone." Dr. Wiebe stands firm in her position that her priority was to honor the wishes of the patient.

Dr. Ellen Wiebe has played a leading role in making sure that all Canadians have equal access to MAiD.

To discuss issues like these and share information about best practices relating to all aspects of medical assistance in dying (MAiD), Dr. Wiebe joined forces with Dr. Stefanie Green to form the Canadian Association of MAiD Assessors and Providers (CAMAP). By engaging in ongoing discussions, CAMAP members hope to ensure that all Canadians have equal access to MAiD under the law and that the process is consistent, properly monitored and well reported.

> "I'm no health care expert, but you've got technology that constantly advances the ability to extend life and maybe improve lifestyle. That puts constant upward pressure on health care costs."

—Steven Burd
Businessman

## — FINANCIAL WORRIES: WHAT DOES IT COST AND SHOULD THAT MATTER? —

**MEDICAL CARE CAN BE EXPENSIVE. WHAT** would happen if physicians made decisions based only on the anticipated costs of treating a patient? Expensive long-term treatment might mean the extension of life for someone who is ill. But if the cost is thought to be too high, would doctors feel pressured to suggest suicide as a more efficient alternative? Or is it reasonable for a society to decide to put a cap on how much we spend on health care? Just because a very expensive treatment is available, does that mean every citizen has an equal right to access that treatment?

## END-OF-LIFE FACT

Medical bills are the single greatest cause of bank-ruptcy in the United States. Approximately 2 million Americans must declare bankruptcy each year after they are unable to pay their medical bills.

In theory, it should not matter whether a medical procedure is costly or not; all people should have access to the same level of care. Unfortunately, the reality is that not everyone can afford all care options, and this can impact end-of-life options for treatment. At some point, might hospitals consider being more permissive about allowing for medically assisted deaths because it's cheaper to allow someone to die than it is to keep them alive with expensive technology?

What happens when an elderly patient develops dementia, a long-term and potentially expensive condition? According to a 2010 study, more than 14 percent of all Americans over the age of seventy-one were suffering from dementia. The cost of caring for these patients was estimated at between $159 billion and $215 billion each year, the bulk of this amount being eaten up by the cost of nursing homes plus formal and informal care.

Who pays for support at the end of life? What if someone would prefer their life savings be given to their loved ones or a favorite charity? Should someone who has been diagnosed with dementia

"If you have principles then you have to act on them. Otherwise, you are just playing games."

—Eike-Henner Kluge

Philosophy professor and ethicist

# Seven

# THE PHILOSOPHY OF DYING

LAW

RELIGION

MEDICINE

Religious beliefs can influence how individuals feel about end-of-life decisions.

**A**SSISTED DYING PUSHES SEVERAL PROFESSIONS OTHER than those in health care to consider whether actions are ethical under various circumstances.

## — ETHICAL CONCERNS —

IT'S HELPFUL TO UNDERSTAND THE DIFFERENCES between ethics, personal conviction, the law and personal choice as we consider who should make the final decision about a person's end-of-life options. We also need to acknowledge that each person involved comes to the table with their own set of biases. Nuala Kenny is a nun, a pediatrician who cares for dying children, a former deputy minister of health, and founder of the Dalhousie University

Department of Bioethics in Nova Scotia. She reminds us that we "can't assume the doctor's and patient's views are consistent." Sometimes an unbiased third party can be very helpful when it comes to sorting out where everyone stands.

Nuala Kenny speaks about her book *Rediscovering the Art of Dying* in Montreal, QC.

*Ethicists* (people who study a branch of philosophy that deals with what is morally right or wrong) can help doctors, hospital administrators, lawyers and individuals understand how our lives (and medical decision-making) have been affected by the recent explosion in medical technology. Ethicists also consider how attitudes are changing in society. They study how such changes impact patient needs and explore the ways in which new information channels (like social media) affect how families share information and organize to advocate for patient rights.

Historically there was one right way to do things based on the law of the land or the dominant religion that dictated right and wrong. Today, though, many religions co-exist alongside *atheists* (who believe there is no God or gods) and *agnostics* (who believe that the existence of God is unknowable). Ethicists are playing a growing role in sorting out the best way to answer tricky questions like those surrounding medically assisted death.

It can be difficult to hear and understand someone else's position, especially when we are talking about an emotionally charged subject like assisted dying. Ethicists can help clarify arguments on all sides.

## — PERSONAL AND EMOTIONAL CONSIDERATIONS —

**EVEN IF THE LAW SAYS THAT** it's okay to decide when you are ready to end your life, many people would still choose not to do so. There are many reasons other than legality that play a role in the decision.

In theory, it may make sense to agree that medically assisted death is the kindest way to help someone avoid terrible suffering at the end of life. But it's quite a different story when you are making the decision yourself or find yourself faced with helping your parent, sibling, friend or child decide whether their suffering and pain outweighs the pleasure and joy of being alive.

There is considerable ongoing discussion about how old a child must be in order to have a full say in treatment options in the case of a terminal illness. One of the current conversations about possible future amendments to Canadian laws involves mature minors (children of at least fourteen who can prove they are able to fully understand the risks and benefits of different treatments). Should competent young people have a say in end-of-life decisions? Each individual comes to this decision with a unique background and, depending on the circumstances, may have a very different reaction to the option of medically assisted death at different points in their life.

Each person also has a unique way of dealing with pain or hard times. Our age can make a difference when it comes to thinking about the end of our life. Family commitments and responsibilities may also play a role in someone's decision to continue to struggle with a long-term disability or terminal illness. Some people are more afraid of death than others.

All of these factors affect the decision as to whether assisted dying is a good choice for a particular person.

## END-OF-LIFE FACT

A recent study found that 70 percent of Canadian millennials (born between 1980 and 2000) believe in life after death. Your beliefs about the afterlife can influence how anxious you feel about dying.

# — RELIGIOUS BELIEFS —

**MOST RELIGIONS CONSIDER LIFE TO BE** the most precious of all gifts and do not condone suicide or assisted dying. The Catholics, for example, believe that God has ownership of the lives of all the creatures on Earth, including people. Most Christians believe a human life is the direct result of God's intervention. Because humans were created by God, it is up to God (and God alone) to decide when each human life should end.

Some Eastern religions, such as Hinduism, see life as an endless cycle of birth, death and rebirth through *reincarnation*. Some believe that suffering is part of life and a way of balancing out bad karma that a person may have accumulated in another lifetime. Deliberately shortening a life may, according to some belief systems, disrupt this process of karmic balancing, forcing the soul

A young woman visits a Hindu temple in Pattadakal, India.

> *"True 'compassion' leads to sharing another's pain; it does not kill the person whose suffering we cannot bear."*
>
> **—Pope John Paul II**
> *Evangelium Vitae 66*

in question to be reborn into more difficult circumstances in the next incarnation.

If you have been raised with a particular set of religious beliefs, this will likely impact your decision-making when approaching death. For example, Pope John Paul II stated that withholding food and fluids is a form of euthanasia by omission and that caregivers are morally obliged to provide food and water by artificial means to a person in a permanent vegetative state. This official church position has an impact on the way in which Catholic hospitals develop end-of-life care policies.

Even if we do not regularly practice a religion in a traditional way (by attending a church, synagogue, temple or mosque, for example), ideas and beliefs held by other members of our family and faith community often shape our own thinking about important life-and-death issues. Because these ideas are so deeply ingrained in us and those around us, it can be hard to imagine other ways of thinking about certain issues.

# — ACTIVISTS HELP DRIVE CHANGE —

**AROUND THE WORLD, VARIOUS RIGHT-TO-DIE SOCIETIES** provide information and guidance to people looking for information about both the law and practical matters relating to ending a life with or without medical assistance. *Final Exit* is a well-known book published in the early 1990s by the Hemlock Society in the United States. The book provides information for those wanting to know exactly how to efficiently and painlessly end their own life.

In Canada, John Hofsess founded the Right to Die Society in 1991. Members of the organization could request help with euthanasia. Hofsess claimed he attended eight deaths, including that of the well-known Canadian poet Al Purdy. In each case he followed a strict protocol to protect himself and his work: he never communicated by email or left any evidence at the location of an assisted suicide. Because it was still illegal to help someone commit suicide, his work had to be conducted in secret or he would have risked being charged with murder or with assisting someone in committing suicide. Though Hofsess believed that it was necessary to provide the service, he also felt a much better option would be to implement some sort of public process with safeguards and protocols. When his assistant, Evelyn

For a number of years before Canada's MAiD legislation came into effect, John Hofsess secretly provided assistance to terminally ill patients wishing to die.

                                        9310 Lochside Dr.,
                                        Sidney, BC V8L 1N6
                                        Apr. 21, '99

John Hofsess,
Evelyn Martens

Dear Both-of-you,

                    Thanks most warmly for your support in my illness.
Follows a brief synopsis of it.  In late Feb. I had a prostate surgery.
This brought on atrial fibrillosis, with conequent drugs to control
it. X-Rays at Saanichton Hospital showed a shadow on my lungs.
A procedure at Vic. Gen. Hos. showed a squamous carcinoma on the
left lung, later confirmed by C.T. Scan.

                                    Dr. Sparling and Dr. Griswold
tell me this can be--probably--removed leaving me with 80% lung
capacity.  However, I believe the massive invasion of my body required
for its removal would very probably kill me (I am now 80 yrs. old).
So that's where I stand right now.

                                    We are busy transferring to my
wife's name what it is feasible to transfer.  She--her name is
Eurithe--refuses to admit that nothing is possible but surgery.
She is exploring other avenues, including Dr. Lam in Vancouver
and possibly Dr. Hoffer in Victoria.  However, various other old
age conditions make it unlikely that my "quality of life" would be
very elevated.

                    And that's where  I stand at this moment.  And I
hesitate to propose my death very strongly in the face of my
wife's resistance.  I'm sure you can see what I mean, and my feeling
in the matter.


          Sincerely,

          *Al Purdy*

          Al Purdy

## Case Studies: Then and Now

IN 1994 AN ELDERLY COUPLE WAS faced with serious health issues. Married for fifty-eight years, Jen and Cecil Bush were struggling to keep going. At eighty-one, Cecil had Alzheimer's disease and was nearly blind. Desperate to end his suffering (Cecil was depressed and asked often to be helped to die), Jen gave him a large dose of sleeping pills and then took what she believed would be enough to kill her too. Both survived the suicide attempt, and several months later Jen tried again, this time stabbing her husband and then herself. Cecil died but Jen survived once again. Jen was found guilty of manslaughter. The judge decided not to send Jen to jail but instead gave her a suspended sentence (she did not have to go to jail).

Twenty-four years later, in 2018, George and Shirley Brickenden faced a similar situation. Married for almost seventy-three years and both in their nineties, the couple suffered from a range of serious illnesses. Under Canada's new law, they were able to request assistance in dying. With their adult children gathered in the room and their favorite music playing, George and Shirley held hands while two doctors injected the lethal doses of medication that ended their lives. Their deaths were peaceful, pain-free and without the trauma of Cecil and Jen's ordeal.

Martens, attended a suicide but was not quite as meticulous as Hofsess, she was charged with assisting in a suicide. She was eventually acquitted because of a lack of evidence. John Hofsess died by assisted suicide in Switzerland at the age of seventy-seven in 2016.

The largest right-to-die group in the world is in Japan. The Japan Society for Dying with Dignity has over 100,000 members, maintains an active website and provides a newsletter, both of which are also available in English.

Lynne Van Luven is a retired professor who volunteers with Dying

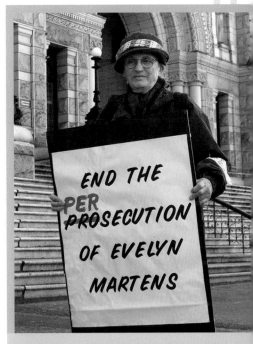

Protesters like Inger Kronseth called for lenience in the case of Evelyn Martens.

With Dignity in Canada. She believes that medically assisted dying should be fully integrated into palliative care treatment options but says, "Not all palliative care administrators agree, so that integration is likely to happen slowly." In Van Luven's opinion, the legislation in Canada does not go far enough. Based on what she hears at Dying With Dignity presentations, she believes that many Canadians want to see the conditions of Alzheimer's disease and other dementias included in Bill C14 (Canada's assisted-dying law). "It's certainly a strongly held view among many...that we do not want to live beyond our mental competence."

"Patients, even those
who are very sick,
think, 'Not me,
not now.'"

———

–Sandra Martin

Author of *A Good Death:
Making the Most of Our Final Choices*

# —Eight—
# THE NATURE OF SUFFERING

**M**ANY PEOPLE ACCEPT THAT AT THE end of a long life, when someone is suffering from a terminal illness, it makes sense to provide whatever measures are necessary to keep that person comfortable and pain-free as they die. Few have a problem with the reality that aggressive pain management may hasten the end of life.

But what about when it's not quite so clear-cut?

What is the one thing we feel would be more than we could bear? For some, unrelenting pain would be unacceptable. For others, paralysis would be unbearable. My mother feared dementia. For my father, an artist his whole life, the fear of becoming blind terrifies him. For others, the loss of independence or the thought of living on for years while fighting crushing fear and anxiety may evoke intense feelings of misery and suffering. When someone is overwhelmed with pain and suffering, when are superhuman efforts to save a life justified? When are they misguided?

It's hard enough to know how we will respond when facing our own serious illness or catastrophic accident. It's even more difficult to try to guess how someone else will feel. For that reason it's simply not possible to enact or enforce strict laws that dictate how and when someone should or should not take control of end-of-life decisions.

I love rock climbing, and the reality is that mountains can be a dangerous environment. The activity of climbing involves some degree of risk, and all climbers know someone who has been killed or seriously injured while doing this sport.

Mountain climbers who have serious accidents may have completely different responses to their injuries and prognoses. For example, Dave Thomson loved climbing and spent as much time as he could in the mountains. A roofer, in 2009 he fell from a roof and broke his spine. He spent three months recovering in hospital and then returned to his home in a wheelchair, unable to walk. For Dave, the loss of his mobility and the reality that he would no longer be able to climb was too much to bear, and he committed suicide only ten days later.

In April 1997, Warren Macdonald found himself pinned under a one-ton boulder during a climbing trip in Australia. After two days he was finally rescued, but the damage done to both his legs was irreparable. His legs had to be amputated mid-thigh. Ten months later he was climbing again, reaching the summit of Cradle Mountain in Tasmania using a modified wheelchair. Warren went

Warren Macdonald likes to say, "Your ideas about yourself determine the course of your life."

> *Each of us feels differently about where we draw the line that determines how much suffering is enough.*

on to become the first above-knee double amputee to climb Mount Kilimanjaro and later El Capitan in Yosemite National Park. Warren, who now lives in Canmore, Alberta, not only climbs mountains; he is also an ice climber, enjoys skiing and is an avid cyclist. A best-selling author and successful motivational speaker, Warren chose to embrace his life and find new ways to do the activities he loves even when confronted with significant challenges.

In describing these two very different reactions to tragic accidents, I'm not suggesting one response is more appropriate or better than the other. We cannot assume that we will ever be able to understand the depth of someone's despair or the fierceness of another person's determination to fight on. In a caring society, those who are facing difficult decisions should be provided with counseling, support, compassion and understanding as well as practical tools (whether for treatment or for painless suicide).

Each of us feels differently about where we draw the line that determines how much suffering is enough. In fact, where we draw that line may change depending on where we are in our lives. A young mother with a new baby may feel that undertaking a course of chemotherapy is worth the side effects if it prolongs her life even a bit. A widower in his eighties may not.

In each situation and for each person we need to consider the physical, psychological and emotional sources of suffering. Philosophical and religious concerns about whether one has lived a good life and what, if anything, comes after death can also be very difficult to resolve, but take on more urgency when someone is facing death. Taking all these dimensions into account is necessary when we try to determine how often medical assistance in dying is actually necessary. Assisted dying may not be needed as often as you might think. In many cases, even a very sick or disabled person is able to access the same suicide options as someone who is otherwise healthy, and they may or may not choose to do so. Even if you are completely paralyzed, it is possible to refuse to eat or receive treatment. Though these may not be quick or efficient ways to end a life, some argue that because these options exist under current laws there is no need to provide a mechanism by which someone else can help speed along a sick person's death.

In democratic societies most people agree with the basic principle of equality for all citizens. Equality for all is a way to make sure a society takes care of everyone's basic needs. If a country decides to make it easier for terminally ill or severely disabled people to have access to lethal drugs and medical assistance when ending a life, then this principle of equality says that the same rights should be offered to anyone who wants to end their life. In most places, committing suicide for reasons other than severe disability or terminal illness is actively discouraged.

# — CHRONIC CONDITIONS —

**LET'S CONSIDER WHAT HAPPENS WHEN SOMEONE** is facing an illness or condition that is chronic, slow, progressive and incurable but not necessarily terminal. In illnesses like Alzheimer's disease, for example, the primary struggle in the early years is with cognitive (mental) function, rather than with physical challenges. Eventually the illness progresses and is fatal, but the period of decline and increasing debilitation may continue for years.

Multiple sclerosis (MS) is a chronic central nervous system condition in which transmission of messages between brain and body is impaired. Symptoms and disease progression vary widely, and while not usually fatal, they can be debilitating. Many people with MS also experience depression. The suicide rate in the MS population is about double the average expected rate.

It's only by looking at the nature of suffering in all its forms that we can begin to decide whether assistance in suicide is justified in cases like these. Is there any way to relieve the suffering? If it doesn't seem so, then strict safeguards need to be put in place in order to prevent errors. A mandatory psychiatric consultation and a significant amount of time between making the request and following through with assistance in dying are intended to reduce the risk of mistakes. This becomes particularly important in the case of hopeless illness or *chronic conditions*.

If someone is paralyzed or unable to swallow medication and has decided after long consideration that suicide is the best choice, then medically assisted dying may be the best option, as long as careful attention has been paid to exhausting other alternatives, and safety protocols have been followed.

## — MENTAL ILLNESS —

SO FAR, WE HAVE TALKED PRIMARILY about physical challenges—serious illnesses and accidents that may make someone wonder whether life is worth living. What about a patient suffering from severe, unrelenting mental illness that does not respond to treatment? If someone suffering from severe depression, for example, is unable to feel any pleasure in life, should we insist that the person carry on? It is hard for anyone who has never been clinically depressed to understand just how bleak and miserable such a life can be. Who, ultimately, has the right to decide whether someone else should keep struggling?

> "Depression is the most painful illness known to man, equalling or exceeding even the most exquisite physical agony."

> —Dr. John Cade
> Psychiatrist

When we talk about depression, we need to distinguish between *situational depression*, which may naturally result from any significant negative life events, and *clinical depression*, which is a persistent, sometimes untreatable mental illness. It's quite normal to feel depressed when confronted with a major change in health or life circumstance, but often counseling and medication can relieve those symptoms and allow a patient to cope with even the most difficult challenges.

Being seriously depressed can lead someone to believe that suicide is the only solution. Ideally, society tries to protect and help people with mental illness. This is one of the reasons why lethal drugs are difficult to obtain and doctors won't help mentally ill patients end their lives. Instead, all efforts are made to protect and treat the person and to prevent them from committing suicide. Nevertheless, many people who suffer from clinical depression or other serious mental illnesses commit suicide, unable to bear the pain of existence.

With two (or more) sets of rules relating to the same act, it becomes very difficult to make sure the sick person is deciding to end their life early because of physical issues and not because

Being seriously depressed can lead someone to believe that suicide is the only solution.

they have become upset or depressed about those physical issues. What if someone who is severely depressed has tried many types of treatment but is not recovering, despite the best efforts of the medical system, community supports and family members? There is a valid argument to be made that this person's quality of life is just as poor as that of someone who has a serious physical ailment. Why should someone with a serious mental illness be stopped from getting access to the same end-of-life options as someone with a serious physical illness?

Most doctors agree that in the case of mental illness, extra safeguards should be put in place. In the Netherlands, after twenty-five years of careful debate, clinical studies and legal test cases, the main criterion for euthanasia was that "the patient's suffering was lasting and unbearable." This description does not exclude assisted dying for a patient with mental illness. In cases like these, a second opinion is required and at least one physician must be a psychiatrist. Part of the assessment includes the doctors considering whether the mental illness is affecting the patient's ability to make an informed decision about assisted dying.

Assisted dying for mentally ill patients continues to be controversial even in places like Belgium and the Netherlands, where it is legal. Two similar cases with different outcomes highlight the challenges unique to mental health patients.

## Case Study: Aurelia and Emily— Mental Illness and Assisted Dying

**A** RESIDENT OF THE NETHERLANDS, TWENTY-NINE-YEAR-OLD Aurelia Brouwers was physically well but fought for the right to die for eight years. She suffered from anxiety and depression, had made several suicide attempts, had been diagnosed with borderline personality disorder and struggled with addictions. She had spent several years in a mental hospital and done time in prison. Brouwers never doubted her decision and wanted to be sure other patients with mental illnesses knew that they, too, had the right to consider euthanasia as an option. She was quite public about her journey and wrote a blog, posted on Facebook and participated in a TV documentary about her death. On January 26, 2018, Brouwers drank a prescribed dose of lethal medication and died quietly soon after.

A

In 2015, twenty-four-year-old Emily, a young Belgian woman, requested and was granted access to medical assistance in dying. After experiencing what she described as unbearable suffering from emotional pain for years, Emily felt the only way to relieve her relentless misery was by dying. Three doctors agreed that her condition was hopeless and untreatable.

During the two weeks before what was supposed to have been her final day, Emily experienced a period of relative calm. At the last moment, she decided not to go ahead with euthanasia. The fact that Emily chose to live raises a number of compelling questions. Did the doctors, by agreeing to her request, actually save her by relieving her anxiety about not having any options? Or were they wrong to agree to grant her request? If Emily experienced such a dramatic change of heart and was able to find a reason to live, does this prove that doctors are fallible and make mistakes? Or does this case show that the system actually provided the support Emily needed to be able to safely explore the option of death and, in the end, choose life?

Dr. Joe Ripperger, a psychiatrist who practices in both the United States and Canada, believes that allowing mentally ill patients access to assisted suicide is troublesome: "I wouldn't be comfortable supporting this for my patients. There is always something else you can try. If I can't help them, then maybe one of my colleagues may be more successful. What if a treatment comes along that would have helped? There are new discoveries being made all the time. It's not a risk I would be willing to take."

The Canadian journalist and mental health advocate Graeme Bayliss disagrees. Having long suffered from depression himself, Bayliss argues in an article published in *The Walrus* that patients suffering from other kinds of illnesses aren't asked to hang on in case a cure might be found at some point. Bayliss believes that the same end-of-life options should be available to anyone suffering from a grave illness, whether that happens to be physical or mental.

## — WHEN YOU NEED HELP TO END YOUR LIFE —

LAWS PREVENTING ASSISTED SUICIDE CAN PLACE friends and family members in a difficult position. In 2011, fifty-one-year-old Bernadette Forde was in the late stages of multiple sclerosis. In Ireland, where Bernadette lived, assisting in a suicide is illegal. Because Bernadette was unable to travel alone to the Dignitas Clinic in Switzerland, her friend Gail O'Rorke agreed to help and go with her. A travel agent reported the plan to police, and Gail O'Rorke was charged with attempting to assist in a suicide. The maximum jail sentence under the law is fourteen years. In the end,

Gail was found not guilty, but the case highlights just how hard it is to know how best to help someone determined to end their life but unable to do so alone.

If being unable to commit suicide alone presents one set of problems (how do you ask for help when helping may land your friend or family member in jail?), planning ahead can be equally challenging.

## Case Study: Robin Williams

**ACTOR AND COMEDIAN ROBIN WILLIAMS NEVER** had the benefit of knowing exactly what was causing the disease that his wife, Susan Schneider Williams, referred to as "the terrorist inside my husband's brain." In addition to physical symptoms eventually attributed to Parkinson's disease, Williams also suffered from increasingly overwhelming paranoia, delusions, panic attacks and depression. Despite making endless visits to doctors, undergoing the most advanced screening tests and desperately trying alternative therapies and medications, his mysterious illness worsened. Overwhelmed and exhausted from fighting his worsening and upsetting symptoms, Robin Williams committed suicide in 2014. It was only after an autopsy and examination of his brain that doctors were able to say that he had been suffering from a particularly severe case of **Lewy body dementia**, a type of brain disease that affects about 1.5 million Americans. Unable to cope with his life being destroyed by a brain he wished he could "reboot," Williams ended his life alone.

*What about if you've been told you have an incurable disease and you decide not to proceed with all possible treatment options?*

What happens, for example, if you have been diagnosed with dementia early enough in the disease process that you're still able to make sound decisions? You may be a little confused and forgetful, but your quality of life might be quite good. Do you make arrangements to commit suicide before things get too bad, or do you take a chance that a loved one will help you later and either not be caught or not be convicted of a crime? I suspect my mother might have committed suicide had she known what was causing her strange mood swings, irrational behavior and odd thinking. But by the time we received a diagnosis she was no longer able to think clearly enough to make such an important decision or put a plan in place to take her own life.

What about if you've been told you have an incurable disease and you decide *not* to proceed with all possible treatment options? Instead, maybe you decide to arrange to end your life sooner rather than later in order to avoid having to go through treatment and its associated risks and side effects.

These are scenarios people face every day, and as laws are being challenged, these dilemmas are discussed publicly more and more often.

# – POPULAR CULTURE AND ASSISTED SUICIDE –

**THESE ONGOING CONVERSATIONS ARE REFLECTED IN** books, TV shows, movies and music. The way in which controversial topics are depicted in popular culture changes over time. Until recently, assisted dying had rarely been shown on TV shows or in movies (with the exception of documentaries). In the Netflix series *Grace and Frankie*, a character named Babe has been battling cancer for some time and has been told her disease has returned. Instead of going through more painful treatments, she is ready to say farewell after she throws one final party. "I'm scared of being a burden, being in pain, and not being myself anymore," Babe says. Her friend Grace suggests that a miracle might be around the corner, but Babe goes ahead with her plans.

*Mary Kills People* is a Canadian TV show about an emergency room doctor who secretly helps terminally ill patients end their lives. When it first aired, both the Catholic Women's League of Canada and the Council of Canadians with Disabilities criticized the show for glamorizing euthanasia.

*Me Before You* is a film based on the novel of the same name by Jojo Moyes. The story follows twenty-six-year-old Louisa Clark, who takes a job as a caretaker for thirty-five-year-old Will Traynor, who was left a quadriplegic after being hit by a motorcycle. Traynor has decided to end his life in Switzerland and, despite enjoying his time with Louisa, goes on to do so. Some disability advocates have criticized the message that severely disabled people might not consider their lives to be worth living.

Lily Tomlin (l) and Jane Fonda (r) play lead characters in the Netflix series *Grace and Frankie*. Though the show is a comedy, it doesn't shy away from more serious topics, like assisted dying.

*Mercy*, a novel by Jodi Picoult, explores themes of love, loyalty and betrayal. In part, the novel follows a court case in which a husband is charged with murder following the mercy killing of his wife. In the novel *Breathless*, author Lurlene McDaniel explores ethical dilemmas and tackles fundamental questions relating to quality of life and who should decide when a life is worth living. Intrigued by the ethical dilemmas posed by euthanasia, McDaniel tackled the subject of assisted suicide from the perspectives of several characters who must decide whether to support the main character's end-of-life wishes. While McDaniel does explore ideas relating to the right to a dignified death, readers may find themselves asking when a request for help crosses the line and becomes selfish.

There's even a British play about assisted dying called *Assisted Suicide: The Musical*, created by Liz Carr, a well-known disability activist, comedian and actress, who has spent a lot of time campaigning against the legalization of assisted dying.

As more cases are discussed and debated publicly in both traditional and social media, we can expect to see more writers, artists, filmmakers and musicians exploring the subject in their work.

## Case Study: Who Was Gillian Bennett?

**O**N AUGUST 18, 2015, EIGHTY-FIVE-YEAR-OLD GILLIAN BENNETT ended her life. She was in the early stages of Alzheimer's disease and did not want to become a burden to her family or to society. In a lengthy blog post, she wrote, "I want out before the day when I can no longer assess my situation, or take action to bring my life to an end…Understand that I am giving up nothing that I want by committing suicide. All I lose is an indefinite number of years of being a vegetable in a hospital setting, eating up the country's money but not having the faintest idea of who I am."

Because Canadian law at the time of Gillian Bennett's death did not allow anyone to help her commit suicide, she had to take care of all the arrangements by herself. Her husband was with her at the end, but could not help in any way. Because of the legal restrictions, Gillian Bennett was put in a position of having to end her life sooner than she might have liked. As her dementia progressed she would not have been able to take the steps necessary to end her life. Because nobody could legally have helped her, she would have spent her final years in a hospital, something she was certain she did not want.

"I think those who have a terminal illness and are in great pain should have the right to choose to end their own life, and those that help them should be free from prosecution."

—Stephen Hawking

Physicist and author

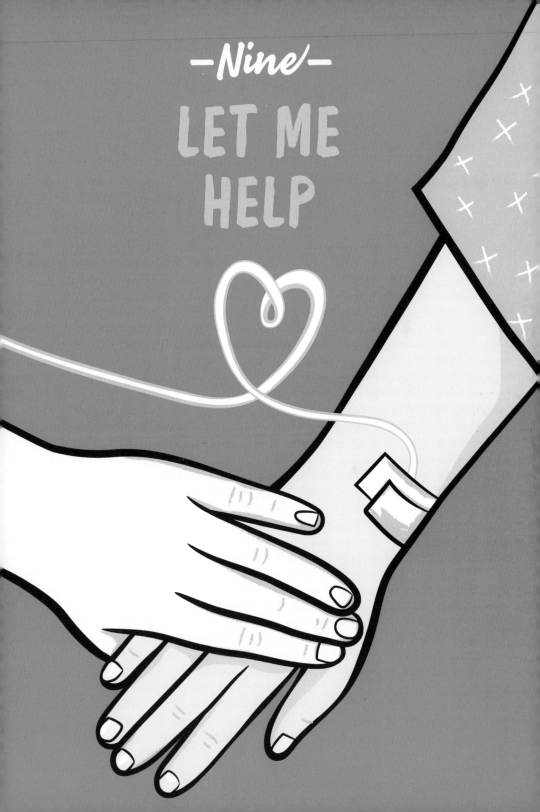

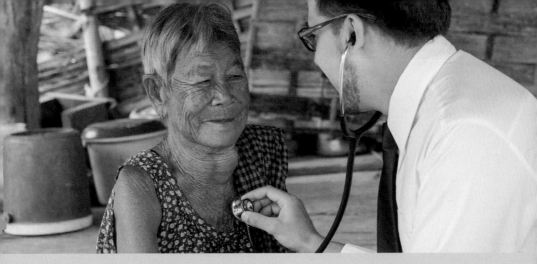

Many people enter the medical profession because they are compassionate. It's important for physicians to remain impartial in the face of a dying patient's choices.

**W**HEN A PERSON BECOMES VERY ILL or old and frail, they need help with many things. If the person is in an institution, that care is generally provided by professionals. Others live at home or with family members, and some or all of the caregiving responsibilities fall to family members.

Infants and children who are ill must also be cared for by others. There are cases where caregivers must make very difficult decisions about when it's appropriate to end a minor's life when a child is suffering from a severe medical condition.

### END-OF-LIFE FACT

Ninety percent of all home care delivered to dying patients is provided by informal caregivers, like family members and friends.

The Terri Schiavo case (see page 23) is an example of how hard it can be to make a decision about what medical attention is appropriate for someone else, whether the person is incapacitated or too young to look after themselves.

In his book *A Good Death*, Dr. Rodney Syme reminds readers that no matter how compelling someone's situation seems, it's "essential that one's innate sympathy for a person's suffering does not introduce bias into one's decisions." In places where medical assistance in dying is legal, it's straightforward to get a second opinion when someone requests help from a doctor. Where it isn't legal, doctors can find themselves in the difficult position of not being able to consult openly with colleagues on challenging cases.

**END-OF-LIFE FACT**

In 2014, 43.5 million Americans served as the primary caregiver for a family member struggling with illness.

## — PARENTS MAKING UNBEARABLE CHOICES —

SOME OF THE MOST HEARTBREAKING EXAMPLES of assisted-dying decisions being made on behalf of others are when parents decide whether a child should be allowed (or helped) to die.

Two examples had very different outcomes.

In 1993 Robert Latimer killed his twelve-year-old daughter Tracy because he could not stand to see her suffering continue. Tracy had

In 1993 Robert Latimer killed his twelve-year-old daughter Tracy. Some accused him of murder, while others considered his act a mercy killing.

a severe form of cerebral palsy and couldn't walk or talk. She had endured many surgeries and experienced a lot of pain. After her death, Latimer was charged with murder and in 1994 was found guilty of second-degree murder. Between then and his eventual release in 2010, Latimer went through several trials and appeals, with courts along the way varying widely in their decisions. Strong positions on both sides (mercy killing versus murder of a disabled person) were expressed in the media, in the courts and around dinner tables across Canada.

In England in 2008, Kay Gilderdale helped her daughter, Lynn, die. At the age of fourteen, Lynn had become ill, and in 1991 she received a diagnosis of myalgic encephalomyelitis (ME), a chronic and disabling disorder. For the next sixteen years Lynn suffered from the effects of the illness. She was hospitalized fifty times and was bedridden and unable to take care of herself. Finally Lynn said, "I'm too broken. You can't fix me any more." Lynn attempted suicide in 2007 but failed. Her resolve was strong, however, and she wrote online, "My body and mind is broken. I'm so desperate to end the never-ending carousel of pain and suffering. I have nothing left and I am spent."

Lynn Gilderdale at age 12, before she fell ill, doing her homework.

Lynn's mother felt torn between respecting her daughter's wishes and wanting to do everything possible to keep her alive. In 2008 Lynn took a large morphine dose, afraid to let her mother help because she was worried about what might happen to her (helping someone to commit suicide was illegal in the United Kingdom at the time). When the morphine did not appear to be working, Kay provided additional medication, and Lynn died.

"I know I did the right thing for Lynn," Kay said in a BBC television documentary. "I had no right to force her to stay and suffer more."

Kay Gilderdale was acquitted after being charged with attempted murder in the death of her daughter Lynn.

The law disagreed, and Kay was charged with attempted murder. Opponents of Kay's decision included Baroness Campbell of Surbiton, Commissioner of the Equality and Human Rights Commission, who said that it's very dangerous to say that under certain circumstances it is right to mercy-kill disabled or terminally ill people. Public opinion, though, supported Kay. In one poll, three out of four people believed friends and relatives should be able to assist in a suicide without fear of prosecution. In the end, Kay Gilderdale was acquitted in a jury trial.

Another case in England received a lot of media attention when doctors at Alder Hey Children's Hospital in Liverpool stated that further treatment of a critically ill toddler was not in the best interests of the child. Twenty-three-month-old Alfie Evans had been in hospital for more than a year and required a ventilator to breathe. His parents wanted to take him to Italy for further treatment, but doctors in England felt that such a trip would not be of any help (scans showed irreparable damage to the little boy's brain).

The case was taken to court, and the parents appealed several times. British law allows the state to intervene when it's felt that a child's needs are not being met. The parents argued that it should

The parents of critically ill child Alfie Evans were denied their request to travel from England to Italy with him.

not be up to the doctors or the courts to decide when caregivers should give up hope. The couple felt that the decision should belong to the parents. But their appeals failed, and Alfie's breathing support was removed. He died a few days later.

Some people believe that children are capable of fully understanding the implications of asking for assistance in dying. In 2002 Belgium became the first country to allow a child's request for euthanasia to be considered. Children must meet the criterion of "constant and unbearable physical or mental suffering that cannot be alleviated." Parents must consent and the child must be evaluated by several physicians, including a child psychiatrist, to ensure that the child fully understands the decision being made.

For parents of a terminally ill child like Alfie Evans, decisions about whether to cease treatment can be excruciating.

**WHEN MY MOTHER'S DEMENTIA PROGRESSED** to a point where she no longer knew where she was and didn't recognize the people around her, including her family, she was also completely dependent on others for care. She was, in some ways, like an infant living in a sixty-two-year-old's body. She wore a diaper, needed someone to feed her, and didn't understand even the simplest conversations. She couldn't read or sing, two activities she had enjoyed throughout her life.

*She couldn't read or sing, two activities she had enjoyed throughout her life.*

By this point in her illness, my mother was in an extended care facility. Eventually she lost the ability to swallow, and our family had to decide whether to provide a feeding tube for her nutrition. Her heart, lungs and kidneys were working well; despite her advanced illness her body was relatively healthy. By providing her with nutrition through a tube we could have kept her going for a while longer.

### END-OF-LIFE FACT

One US study found that 51 percent of dementia patients receive tube feeding.

This family wedding in Bavaria, Germany, was one of the last times that my mother (second from the left) was well enough to travel. Though her behavior on this trip was at times bizarre, it would be several months before she was diagnosed with Pick's disease.

**KNOWING HOW MY MOTHER HAD FELT** about living with dementia, we decided not to provide tube feeding. Through an IV, my mother was provided with medication to keep her sedated so she was unaware of any discomfort during her final days. Her children came from around the world to sit with her. On September 5, 2006, my mother died after having been ill for about seven years.

I am still haunted by my mom's illness and death. I wish we had been able to provide her with a better end. I don't think she would have chosen to spend her final years in an institution, surrounded by strangers. I don't think she would have wanted to live on when she wasn't able to enjoy her family and the activities that had always meant so much to her. I don't think she would have wanted to cause those she loved so much grief and hurt in the years when we tried to care for her at home. But at the time, we did not have the option of assisting her with suicide. Even though in the haze of her confusion she would often say things like "If I had a sword I would fall on it and die," there was no practical way to decide whether she was hallucinating or if she genuinely wanted to end her life. And even if, as I suspect, that would have been her choice, we had no legal, practical way to help her. I was not as brave as some others have been and was not prepared to test the law by illegally providing my mother with an overdose when I had the chance. I had a child of my own to raise and was afraid that if I were convicted of murder, my daughter would have to face not only the loss of her grandmother but also a life with her mother in jail.

Sadly, for patients with dementia, the law—even in places like the Netherlands that have relatively inclusive assisted dying laws—does not permit access to assisted suicide for someone who is unable to prove their mental competence. Though **advance directives** are supposed to provide guidance to physicians, when push comes to shove, few doctors are willing to agree to provide a medically assisted death for a dementia patient who has passed the point where they are able to provide **informed consent**. Even if my mother had fallen ill today, Canada's law as currently written would not have helped, though the changing social and legal climate might have further reduced the chances that I would have been prosecuted if I had ended her life.

I don't think she would have wanted to live on when she wasn't able to enjoy her family and the activities that had always meant so much to her.

My mother, third from the right, enjoying one of the last trips she was able to make with her family.

"As believers, how can we fail to see that abortion, euthanasia and assisted suicide are a terrible rejection of God's gift of life and love? And as believers, how can we fail to feel the duty to surround the sick and those in distress with the warmth of our affection and the support that will help them always to embrace life?"

—Pope John Paul II

(1999)

"Patients who are being kept alive by technology and want to end their lives already have a recognized constitutional right to stop any and all medical interventions, from respirators to antibiotics. They do not need physician-assisted suicide or euthanasia."

—Ezekiel Emanuel
Oncologist and bioethicist

**A**S LAWS IN SOME PLACES ARE changed to make assisted dying legal, critics express concerns that vulnerable people (children, the elderly, people living with disabilities) will suffer as a result. Another fear is that if it is easier to die, more people will take advantage of this option, even when it isn't really necessary. Opponents of assisted dying are worried that if euthanasia is legalized, investment in palliative care will decline. Though these concerns have not been borne out, it is important to make sure that adequate precautions are taken to prevent actual abuses of new laws.

# — PROTOCOLS AND SAFEGUARDS —

**WHEREVER ASSISTED DYING HAS BEEN LEGALIZED,** strict rules and regulations about who should be allowed to have access to this option have been put in place to help prevent abuse. The following is a summary of the rules and restrictions that are in place in Oregon. Similar rules and restrictions have been put in place wherever assisted dying has been legalized.

1. The person seeking assistance with dying must be an adult (over eighteen years of age) and a resident of Oregon.

2. The person must be terminally ill with less than six months to live.

3. The person must be mentally competent and able to make their own medical decisions.

4. The origin of the request must be thoroughly explored to eliminate the possibility of pressure or influence from others.

5. The person must make a written request for the medication. The request must be witnessed by two other people.

6. The person must be evaluated by two different doctors.

7. The person must be experiencing intolerable suffering.

8. The desire to receive assistance must be consistent over time. Multiple requests must be made.

9. Where a physician feels it to be necessary, a psychiatric assessment should be done to ensure mental competence.

10. If the person is approved and is given a prescription for lethal medication, he or she must be able to self-administer the medication (the doctor does not give the lethal dose).

11. The person must be informed of any other alternatives, including palliative care.

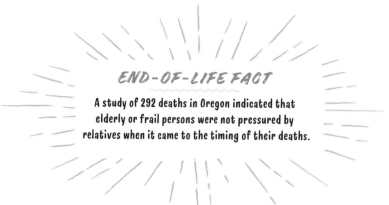

### END-OF-LIFE FACT

A study of 292 deaths in Oregon indicated that elderly or frail persons were not pressured by relatives when it came to the timing of their deaths.

ONE OF THE WAYS WE CAN prevent abuse or manipulation of those nearing the end of life is to ensure that the final act (taking medication, for example) remains the responsibility of the patient. This precludes friends, family or physicians from helping directly, but in many cases, just knowing we have control over the timing of our death reduces anxiety and psychological distress. This restriction on access is important for some who fear that easier access to assisted dying will eventually lead to an increase in involuntary euthanasia.

Members of the Euthanasia Prevention Coalition believe that giving doctors the right to cause the death of patients will never be safe and that no "so-called safeguards" will protect those who are most vulnerable. According to the National Council on Aging, about one in ten Americans over the age of sixty has experienced some form of elder abuse. In more than half the reported cases, the perpetrator is a family member (often an adult child or spouse).

The Euthanasia Prevention Coalition believes that making it easier to obtain assistance in dying will result in an increase in inappropriate requests from those already suffering from elder abuse. They believe there will always be people who will abuse the power to cause death and there will always be more reasons to hasten death. According to the organization, assisted dying creates new paths for abuse of elders, people with disabilities and other marginalized people and represents an abandonment of people who live with mental illness who require support and care.

## — DEBATE AMONG DISABILITY ADVOCATES —

**SOME PEOPLE WITH DISABILITIES HAVE BEEN** vocal opponents of medical assistance in dying. But this position is not held by all people with disabilities. The Alliance of People with Disabilities Who Are Supportive of Legal Assisted Dying Society says it's wrong to equate disability with vulnerability. People with disabilities are capable of making rational, voluntary and autonomous decisions to hasten their own deaths. The group's position in favor of assisted dying argues that it's unfair to deprive an entire class of persons (who may be unable to end their lives without help) of the ability to legally access assistance.

To those who err on the side of caution and oppose legalized assisted death, the risk of abusing new laws is greater than any

Incarcerated populations may be at risk of abuse by those in power unless adequate human-rights protection is in place. At Willowbrook State School, children in residence were treated unethically.

potential benefits. Strict laws, it's argued, serve to protect the most vulnerable members of society and should not be watered down.

Sadly, there *have* been cases throughout history when vulnerable people have been victimized and abused. Some of these crimes were committed by doctors. During World War II, doctors working with the Nazis performed thousands of medical experiments on prisoners being held in concentration camps. Drug tests, surgical procedures, and experiments that involved observing how different people reacted when deliberately infected with diseases caused terrible suffering and sometimes death. Between 1956 and the 1970s, students with developmental disabilities at Staten Island's Willowbrook State School in New York were deliberately infected with hepatitis, which resulted in serious sickness and suffering. Other institutions, like prisons, mental institutions and Indian residential schools, have likewise used residents for ethically questionable medical experiments and studies.

Though these rare examples of physicians behaving inappropriately are horrifying, the vast majority of medical personnel do not abuse their patients. Providing clear limits and guidelines is intended to prevent anyone from taking advantage of new laws.

## — EUGENICS: COULD THE WEAKEST BE AT RISK? —

**IN THE MOST EXTREME FORM OF** abuse, non-voluntary euthanasia could be used by unscrupulous individuals interested in practicing *eugenics* (the science of improving a human population by controlled breeding). By restricting who is able to have children (by forcing sterilization, for example) or cutting short "undesirable" lives, those who believe in trying to improve the genetics of a group of people could find sympathetic doctors to euthanize individuals not considered to be worthy of living.

In my own family, the Nazi policies relating to creating a perfect race of healthy Germans

> ✳ *Euthanasia* ✳ *could be used by unscrupulous individuals* ✳ *interested in practicing eugenics.* ✳

Human-rights abuses were rampant during the years when Nazi Germany's power was at its greatest. Here, members of the League of German Girls demonstrate the ideal of physical perfection promoted by Nazi Germany.

struck close to home. When my mother was an infant in Germany, she contracted polio and was left partially paralyzed on one side. Nazi doctors made my grandmother sign a document stating that if the polio worsened and affected her daughter's brain, she would bring my mother back to be euthanized. Fortunately, my grandmother was never forced to make that decision, but I understand the concerns of those who worry that people with the power to do so could take advantage of easy access to lethal medications and more relaxed euthanasia laws. Linking euthanasia to eugenics is one reason why there has been so much resistance to wide adoption of medically assisted death.

# — UNDERLYING ASSUMPTIONS —

**ONE OF THE UNDERLYING ASSUMPTIONS ABOUT** why we would want to make assisted dying an acceptable option for people with serious illnesses or disabilities is that these two conditions are considered to be bad enough that dying may be a "better" alternative. Is that a fair assumption?

There are other circumstances in which someone may be experiencing truly awful suffering, and yet suicide is not considered to be a viable option. A prisoner who is serving a life sentence for a terrible crime may suffer from serious depression and face decades of misery in solitary confinement, but the prison system will go to great lengths to prevent that person from ending their life. Why? One could argue that it's just as unlikely that the prisoner will ever return to a normal, healthy, happy life as someone with a terminal illness. It's very expensive to keep someone in jail for decades. Should the cost of housing prisoners who can never be reformed be a factor when deciding whether to let someone die? Why should assisted dying not be an option in a case like this?

*Should the cost of housing prisoners who can never be reformed be a factor when deciding whether to let someone die?*

## — SLIPPERY SLOPE —

**SOME PEOPLE BELIEVE THAT CONDONING A** doctor's actions when a patient's death is hastened without the patient's explicit consent (for example, when a doctor decides to provide terminal sedation to someone in a coma) is just the first step toward more sinister practices. In the strictest sense, opponents of any form of assisted dying would say that the care my grandmother received was inappropriate and could result in the death of those less seriously ill or not quite as close to death.

## — PLANNING AHEAD —

**AFTER GIVING A LOT OF THOUGHT** to end-of-life issues, it's a good idea to prepare an advance directive. This is a document that clearly describes what treatment a person does or does not want in the case of a future medical event where they are unable to express their wishes.

Something that may be spelled out in an advance directive is the desire to refuse treatment in the case of a catastrophic event. For example, let's say a person has suffered non-reversible brain injuries in a serious accident, and surgery may prolong their life; the accident victim might prefer not to accept the lifesaving treatment but is unable to express these wishes. A clear advance directive would provide some guidance for family and caregivers in this case.

Some people have gone so far as to have *DNR* tattooed on their chest. Standing for *Do Not Resuscitate*, the letters are intended to prevent first responders, bystanders or medical professionals from performing CPR if the person is found unconscious.

The idea of advance directives is great, but very few people have them. And even when a DNR order is in place, the document often doesn't make it to the patient's chart. Also problematic is the fact that people's choices and desires change based on altered diagnoses and treatment options and where they find themselves in life. People may choose to stay alive for milestone birthdays, weddings or significant holidays even when they are desperately ill. It's a major challenge to create an advance directive that can predict how someone will feel during a stressful, complicated situation that can change by the minute.

## — GOOD DECISIONS BASED ON FACTS —

ONE WAY TO ENSURE THAT PATIENTS and families make fully informed decisions is to make sure they receive all the information they need about the likely course of an illness. This can be challenging. Sometimes the amount of stress and anxiety that surrounds a serious illness makes it impossible to properly absorb and process large amounts of complicated medical information. Often there is more than one way to treat an illness or manage a longer-term disability. There can be many options on the table, and it can be hard to figure out what the best treatment options might be. Patients may also find themselves facing the challenge of researching new or alternative treatments that have not been offered by medical professionals. If all the options are not presented and discussed, it could be easy to jump to the conclusion that there is no hope or that assisted dying is the best solution. In some cases, it may be the easiest solution, but it may not be the only or best solution.

Soumya Karlamangla, health reporter for the *Los Angeles Times*, notes that one of the unexpected benefits of California's medically assisted death law is that health-care workers are now having conversations with patients that are "leading to patients' fears and needs regarding dying being addressed better than ever before."

## What Is Informed Consent?

BEFORE PERFORMING ANY MEDICAL PROCEDURE, PATIENTS are asked to give informed consent. This means the patient must be told about all the possible risks, consequences and benefits of any proposed treatment. Only after a patient fully understands all the pros and cons of a particular procedure are they able to agree to give their informed consent.

In terms of assisted dying, informed consent means the patient needs to be told of all treatment and palliative care options as well as the risks of assisted death (including the risks associated with the medications and the process of administering them).

## The Conversation Project

**I**N NORTH AMERICA WE ARE VERY reluctant to talk about death and dying. Ellen Goodman says this must change. She is the co-founder of the Conversation Project. She says, "Have these conversations [about end of life care and how you would like to die] at the kitchen table, rather than in a crisis." The Conversation Project is dedicated to helping people talk about their wishes for end-of-life care. A free online kit at *theconversationproject.org* includes questions to think about before having a conversation with loved ones, as well as some tips for planning when and where to start chatting (and with whom). Whether you write your wishes down or appoint someone to speak for you, communicating your preferences to those closest to you is really important.

## — APPOINTING A PROXY —

ANOTHER OPTION SOME PEOPLE PREFER IS to appoint a *health care proxy* (or *surrogate*), someone who will speak on the patient's behalf if they are too ill to participate in medical decision-making. Obviously this is a position of huge trust and not a responsibility to be taken lightly. Patients who choose this option must take the time to fully discuss their wishes and make sure that their chosen representative understands what they would want under different circumstances. According to the Canadian Virtual Hospice, it's a good idea to name your chosen proxy in your advance directive.

**END-OF-LIFE FACT**

Ninety percent of people say that talking with their loved ones about end-of-life care is important. Only 2 percent have actually done so. (Conversation Project national survey, 2013)

## — MEDICINE: ART OR SCIENCE? —

EVEN WHEN WE KNOW EXACTLY WHAT'S wrong with someone, it's difficult to predict how long they will live with a terminal disease or how much suffering they will endure. Some people go into *remission* (their disease simply stops progressing) and are able to enjoy many more months or years of quite functional life beyond what their doctor has told them is likely. In other cases, the end of life comes much more quickly than anticipated.

Part of the challenge when helping a patient make an appropriate end-of-life decision is knowing how much and what type of information the patient will need.

*Even when we know exactly what's wrong with someone, it's difficult to predict how long they will live.*

## Death Cafés

**D**EATH CAFÉS ARE INFORMAL GROUPS THAT meet to talk about death and dying. Started in England and now springing up all over the world, these discussion groups are organized for and attended by anyone who has an interest in talking about death and dying.

For many who are diagnosed with a terminal illness, it's quite normal to experience complex feelings associated with grieving. Denial and numbness, anger, bargaining, relief, sadness and depression are all natural reactions to receiving devastating news, and no two people respond in exactly the same way. Communicating feelings, reaching out to family and friends, counseling, and sometimes treatment for depression (like medication) can all help someone cope with a serious diagnosis. Eventually the patient may experience acceptance. With adequate management of symptoms and proper pain relief, it's possible for them to live out their days without feeling the need to request assistance in dying.

"You needn't die happy when your time comes, but you must die satisfied, for you have lived your life from the beginning to the end..."

---

—Stephen King

Author

# -Eleven-
# A GOOD DEATH

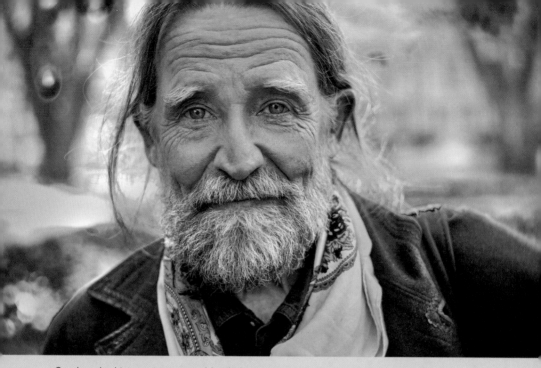

Stephen Jenkinson encourages North Americans to look hard at their relationship with death.

## — ANGEL OF DEATH —

**S**TEPHEN JENKINSON HAS BEEN AT THE bedside of so many dying patients he has been called the Angel of Death. For years he was the leader of the palliative care counseling team at Toronto's Mount Sinai Hospital. He believes that death is what makes us human and that it is the most important thing to shape our lives.

"It is not human to fear death," Jenkinson says, pointing out that other cultures have a different relationship with the end of life than most of us in North America. Jenkinson believes we should consider acknowledging death from the start of life. "Life requires death to be able to continue. Death feeds everything that lives," he points out.

So what does a good death look like early in the twenty-first century? As we have discussed, not that long ago dying took place at home. Family members cared for the sick and, after death, washed the body and dressed the deceased for burial. Visitors came to say good-bye and share stories. Community members and friends provided comfort along with food and drink and sometimes music and song, acknowledging both life and loss.

In some parts of the world, these kinds of death ceremonies and rituals are still the norm. In North America, the reality is that most people die in institutions where, typically, space is at a premium. After a patient dies the body is removed quite quickly and there is little time to sit with death. Rituals relating to the care of the dead body have mostly been handed over to professionals.

People like Brandy Gallagher of O.U.R. Ecovillage on Vancouver Island in British Columbia feel that the process of dying should be brought home again, that death is a natural part of life and should not be relegated to a hospital room. In the past, she recalls, "Grandma's bed was brought into the kitchen. She was at the centre of what was going on. She never left life to die."

At O.U.R. Ecovillage, a hand-built structure called the Sanctuary is used for end-of-life care. There's enough room for families to stay throughout the dying process, and medical

One of the uses of the Sanctuary at O.U.R. Ecovillage on Vancouver Island is to provide a quiet, beautiful space for people coming to the end of their lives.

## Euthanasia Coaster

**E**UTHANASIA COASTER IS A PIECE OF conceptual art by Julijonas Urbonas. This once-in-a-lifetime ride was designed to kill all the passengers aboard so their final experience is a death of "elegance and euphoria." The design would, in theory, take passengers up more than 1,600 feet (500 meters) before a drop that would reach 310 miles per hour (500 kilometers per hour) before entering a series of loops. At that speed, the g-forces would be enough to deprive the passengers' brains of oxygen. Though the ride is not meant to be built, the concept is rather intriguing. Will our society ever become so comfortable with death and dying that a ride like this might one day be available?

*END-OF-LIFE FACT*

In Switzerland, DIGNITAS reports that 70 percent of those who are eligible for assisted dying do not take advantage of it.

personnel can come and go as needed. If desired, a doctor can provide medical assistance in dying. At O.U.R. Ecovillage it's also possible to arrange to have a loved one's ashes scattered in green burial grounds on site.

Re-teaching the lost art of dying is important to Brandy. She helps organize workshops run by organizations like Canadian Integrative Network for Death Education and Alternatives (CINDEA).

## — WHO IS IN CHARGE HERE? —

**ONE OF THE CONSIDERATIONS THAT COMES** up in discussions about assisted dying is who should take on this responsibility. Some feel that doctors are the logical professionals, if death is considered a natural part of life and something everybody will eventually face. Others believe that doctors who help patients die are in a ***conflict of interest***. A physician's primary job should be treating and, where possible, healing people, not ending lives.

As societal attitudes toward the end of life shift, new roles emerge for those who can guide terminally ill patients and their families in the process of dying.

Some think it's time for a new job entirely, a euthanist who would be specially trained to administer the correct dose of a deadly combination of drugs for those who qualify at the end of life. Other professionals like **death midwives** or **death doulas** and **end-of-life ceremony leaders** would help guide dying individuals and their families through the process of dying.

We all hope that, when the time comes, we'll have time to fulfill our last wishes and make sure our affairs are in order. With luck, our relationships have been repaired or strengthened as death approaches. Instead of a sense of panic and confusion, we hope dying can be a time of calmness and peace for all involved. It would be lovely to think that the final days and hours of a person's life would be a time of celebration and joy rather than grief and regret.

## Case Study: John Shields

SEVENTY-EIGHT-YEAR-OLD JOHN SHIELDS SUFFERED FROM AMYLOIDOSIS, an incurable disease that causes serious nerve damage and eventually may compromise major organs and cause irreversible damage to the heart, kidneys, liver and nervous system. John's doctor, Stefanie Green, agreed that he qualified for medical assistance in dying.

Mr. Shields chose a date for his death, and the evening before, he and his wife, Robin, organized a party in his hospice room in Victoria, British Columbia. Friends and family members gathered to share stories, sing, eat (take-out chicken) and drink, celebrating Mr. Shields's life and his many connections and accomplishments. The next day Dr. Green, who believes that helping people die when they are ready is "on the continuum of care of helping people," arrived with four syringes, each containing a different medication used in the process of euthanasia.

Mr. Shields's wife, stepdaughter and a few close friends were at his side, and after a final few words, some singing and a special ritual, Dr. Green asked if he was ready. He said he was. The injected medications took only minutes to work, first sending Mr. Shields into a deep sleep and then stopping his heart.

## Sarco

**D**ESIGNED BY **DR. PHILIP NITSCHKE**, the assisted dying activist and director of Exit International, Sarco is a capsule designed to provide the user with a reliable, peaceful death. To make it as easy as possible for people to access this technology, the device is to be made by a 3D printer. Using liquid nitrogen, the capsule deprives the user of oxygen. Unconsciousness and death are the result. The top part of the unit is made from 100 percent biodegradable materials and can be used as a coffin. Sarco is portable, so it can be set up wherever the dying person wishes to end their life.

For security, each Sarco will have a coded keypad that must be unlocked prior to use. In order to get the code, the user will have to follow an online application procedure to ensure that all legal requirements are met and that they are fully aware of all the implications of using the device. The plans for printing the device are not yet available, but as 3D printing technology continues to develop and becomes more widely available and affordable, the developers hope Sarco becomes a viable option for those who meet legal requirements.

Yes, there should also be space for sadness and grieving, but lots of people believe that death, like life, can be a much more balanced experience than it currently is for many.

As you first read in the introduction, the first step toward shifting our ideas about dying and the end of life is accepting that death comes to all of us.

My hope is that this book will encourage you to begin to have conversations about death and the way we die and, just as importantly, about how we live our lives. In the course of researching this book I have thought long and hard about death and dying—my own death and the deaths of those I care most about. Yes, at times I've felt sad thinking about death and loss, but I've also come to appreciate in a new and deeper way what a gift it is to be alive.

I've always tried to live well, to be content, to love and look after those closest to me, but now I am also thinking about how important it is to die well too. I am in no rush to get to the end, but when it comes, I hope I will meet death in comfort, surrounded by loved ones, knowing I have lived as well and as fully as possible.

Even as a child, my mother was strong-willed and knew her own mind. She would have been pleased to see that Canada has now provided terminally ill patients with options not available when she and my omi (her mother) were sick.

# *Acknowledgments*

"**IF I EVER LOSE MY MIND** to dementia, take me out back and shoot me."
Little did I know how influential my mother's words would prove to
be. This book would likely not have been written had she not repeated
that phrase so often when I was a teenager and then gone on to develop
exactly the illness she had so feared. I owe my mother a debt of gratitude
for always being so outspoken and opinionated and for always encouraging me to find my own voice as a writer. The rest of my family deserves
mention here as well. Not only have they been staunch supporters of
my work, but they have provided emotional and practical support when
needed as well, always with good humor and kindness. I am lucky to have
the family I do. My partner, Fabio, has also been an essential member
of my support crew, not only providing steady, everyday encourage-
ment but also indulging me in conversations about death, dying and
the medical profession.

Over the course of researching this book, I've spoken with many
medical people, family members of the dead and dying, and others
involved with end-of-life care in various capacities, and I have been
impressed with and encouraged by the level of thoughtful conversation around this topic. My heartfelt thanks go out to those who agreed
to speak with me about a subject that is so intensely personal and, at
the same time, of universal interest. The whole team at Orca Book
Publishers has, as usual, been fantastic to work with, but special thanks
must go out to my editor Sarah Harvey, who has believed in this project
from the very beginning. As always, her sharp eye, probing questions,
and links to yet more articles, films and books made this book much
better than anything I could have managed to write without her guidance and suggestions.

# Glossary

**active euthanasia:** death occurs after an act is committed (e.g., a lethal dose of drugs is given)

**acute care:** short-term, intensive treatment following a severe injury or serious illness

**advance directive:** a written statement describing the type of medical care desired in the event that a person is unable to communicate with medical professionals

**agnostic:** a person who believes it is impossible to know whether God exists

**assisted dying, assisted suicide:** a suicide in which the act is committed with another person's help

**atheist:** a person who does not believe in the existence of God

**brain-dead:** total lack of brain activity, including that needed to sustain basic life systems (like respiration)

**cardiopulmonary resuscitation (CPR):** a procedure for keeping someone alive that involves pressing on the chest to keep blood flowing through the heart, often combined with blowing air into the mouth

**chronic condition:** a long-lasting, persistent health condition that continues for months or years

**clinical depression:** a prolonged and persistent state of severe depression

**coma:** an unconscious state in which a person does not respond to light, sound or painful stimuli

**conflict of interest:** when a person has two different (sometimes opposing) loyalties or interests that make it difficult or impossible to reach an objective decision

**death doula, death midwife:** a trained, experienced professional who helps during the dying process

**dementia:** a group of symptoms related to chronic deterioration of the brain, often affecting memory, judgment, personality, language and reasoning

**divine intervention:** an event that occurs as the result of a deity's action

**Do Not Resuscitate (DNR) order:** an advance request that extreme medical measures not be taken in order to prolong life

**double effect:** if the primary intention of a medical intervention is to relieve pain and suffering but the secondary effect may be to hasten death, the intervention is said to have a double effect

**end-of-life ceremony leader:** a trained individual who specializes in assisting someone near death and their loved ones in arranging and sometimes performing special rituals near the time of death

**ethicist:** a person who studies a branch of philosophy that deals with what is morally right or wrong and how to implement moral decisions in real-world situations

**eugenics:** the practice of selective breeding and euthanasia for the purpose of improving the genetic makeup of a population

**euthanasia:** the termination of a patient's life when the patient is suffering from an incurable illness

**health care proxy, health care surrogate:** an individual appointed to make medical decisions on behalf of someone incapable of doing so because of incapacitation (may also refer to the document that names such an agent)

*Hippocratic Oath:* an oath historically taken by physicians that outlines the ethical responsibilities of the medical profession

*hospice:* a facility for those who are terminally ill

*informed consent:* permission granted to a medical professional after all the pros and cons of a treatment have been presented, discussed and considered

*IV drip:* medication or fluids delivered through a needle inserted into a vein

*Lewy body dementia:* a particular type of degenerative brain disease associated with protein deposits known as Lewy bodies

*life support:* specialized equipment used to emulate essential body functions such as respiration when a person is extremely ill

*management of terminal anguish:* sedation and comfort measures taken to relieve symptoms of anxiety and pain as a patient nears the end of life

*manslaughter:* killing another person without advance planning or malice

*medical assistance in dying (MAiD):* a death that occurs with the assistance of a physician and at the request of the patient

*medically assisted death, medically assisted suicide:* a death that occurs with the indirect assistance of a physician and at the request of the patient

*morphine:* a powerful opiate used for pain management

*opioid:* a type of drug that is used to treat extreme pain, derived from the opium poppy

*palliative care:* a medical specialty that focuses on treating patients as they approach death

*palliative sedation, terminal sedation:* the deliberate induction of a state of oblivion or unconsciousness to ease pain or distress as death approaches

*passive euthanasia:* death occurs as the result of an act of omission; death is allowed to occur

*permanent vegetative state, persistent vegetative state:* a state of unawareness of self and surroundings, in which the patient is able to breathe without assistance and which usually follows severe traumatic brain injury

*pharmacological oblivion:* a state of unawareness or unconsciousness brought about by administration of medication

*physician-assisted suicide:* a death that occurs with the indirect assistance of a physician and at the request of the patient

*premeditated murder:* the illegal killing of one person by another

*reincarnation:* the belief that the soul returns to a new physical body after a person dies

*remission:* a temporary reduction in the seriousness of an illness in which symptoms may disappear or be reduced

*sedative:* a medication used to induce sleep or relaxation

*situational depression:* a short-term form of depression experienced as a result of a stressful or traumatic event

*stimulant:* a medication used to induce wakefulness or increase the level of nervous activity in the body

*terminal illness:* a sickness likely to result in a person's death

*tuberculosis:* a contagious disease caused by bacteria, which often affects the lungs

*voluntary euthanasia:* ending a life painlessly in accordance with a patient's wishes

**163**

# ✳ References ✳

*Print*

Anonymous. "It's Over, Debbie." *Journal of the American Medical Association*. January 1988.

Bauslaugh, Gary. *The Right to Die: The Courageous Canadians Who Gave Us the Right to a Dignified Death*. Toronto, ON: Lorimer, 2016.

*Bow Valley Crag and Canyon*. "Collection to Honour Dave Thomson." Banff, AB: June 1, 2011.

Butler, Katy. *Knocking on Heaven's Door: The Path to a Better Way of Death*. New York: Simon & Schuster, 2013.

Cebuhar, Jo Kline. *The Practical Guide to Health Care Advance Directives*. West Des Moines, IA: Murphy, 2015.

Close, Lesley, and Jo Cartwright, eds. *Assisted Dying: Who Makes the Final Decision? The Case for Greater Choice at the End of Life*. London: Peter Owen, 2014.

Colby, William H. *Unplugged: Reclaiming Our Right to Die in America*. New York: AMACOM, 2006.

Cook, Hyran. *Responsible Suicide: The Courage to Do What You've Got to Do*. Cinda Park, South Africa: Principle Press, 2015.

Eddy, David M. "A Conversation with My Mother." *Journal of the American Medical Association* 272 (1994): 179–181.

Eisenberg, Jon B. *The Right vs. the Right to Die: Lessons from the Terri Schiavo Case and How to Stop It from Happening Again*. New York: Harper Collins, 2005.

Falconer, Tim. *That Good Night: Ethicists, Euthanasia and End-of-Life Care*. Toronto, ON: Penguin Canada, 2009.

Friedman, Laurie S. *Assisted Suicide*. San Diego, CA: ReferencePoint Press, 2009.

Gorsuch, Neil M. *The Future of Assisted Suicide and Euthanasia*. Princeton, NJ: Princeton University Press, 2009.

Humphry, Derek. *Final Exit: The Practicalities of Self-Deliverance and Assisted Suicide for the Dying* (digital edition). 2011.

Kiernan, Stephen P. *Last Rights: Rescuing the End of Life from the Medical System*. New York: St. Martin's Press, 2006.

Kluge, Eike-Henner. *Ethics in Healthcare: A Canadian Focus*. Toronto, ON: Pearson, 2012.

Lavi, Shai J. *The Modern Art of Dying: A History of Euthanasia in the United States*. Princeton, NJ: Princeton University Press, 2009.

Martin, Sandra. *A Good Death: Making the Most of Our Final Choices*. Toronto, ON: HarperCollins, 2016.

McDaniel, Lurlene. *Breathless*. New York: Random House, 2009.

Meilaender, Gilbert. *Should We Live Forever? The Ethical Ambiguities of Aging*. Grand Rapids, MI: William B. Eerdmans, 2013.

Mitchell, John B. *Understanding Assisted Suicide: Nine Issues to Consider; A Personal Journey*. Ann Arbor, MI: University of Michigan Press, 2007.

Oliver, David B. *Exit Strategy: Depriving Death of Its Strangeness* (self-published, Smashwords, 2013).

Ostaseski, Frank. *The Five Invitations: Discovering What Death Can Teach Us about Living Fully.* New York: Flatiron Books, 2017.

Pope John Paul II. *A Pilgrim Pope: Messages for the World.* Kansas City, MO: Andrews McMeel, 1999.

Preston, Thomas A. "Physician Involvement in Life-Ending Practices." *Seattle University Law Review* 18, no. 531 (1995).

Shepherd, Lois. *If That Ever Happens to Me: Making Life and Death Decisions after Terri Schiavo.* Chapel Hill, NC: University of North Carolina Press, 2009.

Smith, Fran, and Sheila Himmel. *Changing the Way We Die: Compassionate End of Life Care and the Hospice Movement.* Berkeley, CA: Cleis Press, 2013.

Smith, Wesley J. *Forced Exit: Euthanasia, Assisted Suicide, and the New Duty to Die.* New York: Encounter Books, 2006.

Steffen, Lloyd, and Dennis R. Cooley. *The Ethics of Death: Religious and Philosophical Perspectives in Dialogue.* Minneapolis, MN: Fortress Press, 2014.

Sumner, L.W. *Assisted Death: A Study in Ethics and Law.* Oxford, England: Oxford University Press, 2011.

Syme, Rodney. *A Good Death: An Argument for Voluntary Euthanasia.* Carlton, Australia: Melbourne University Press, 2008.

Syme, Rodney. *Time to Die.* Carlton, Australia: Melbourne University Press, 2016.

Torr, James D. *Euthanasia* (Opposing Viewpoints Series). San Diego, CA: Greenhaven Press, 2000.

Tulloch, Gail. *Euthanasia: Choice and Death.* Edinburgh, Scotland: Edinburgh University Press, 2006.

Warraich, Haiden. *Modern Death: How Medicine Changed the End of Life.* New York: St. Martin's Press, 2017.

Zucker, Marjorie B. *The Right to Die Debate: A Documentary History.* Westport, CT: Greenwood Press, 1999.

### Online

Alzheimer Society of Canada. "Dementia Numbers." alzheimer.ca/en/nb/About-dementia.

American Academy of Hospice and Palliative Medicine. "Statement on Physician-Assisted Dying." June 24, 2016. aahpm.org/positions/pad.

Arnold, Elizabeth Mayfield. "Factors That Influence Consideration of Hastening Death among People with Life-Threatening Illnesses." *Health and Social Work* 29, no. 1 (2004): 17+. questia.com/read/1G1-112986550/factors-that-influence-consideration-of-hastening.

BC Civil Liberties Association. "Robyn Moro, a Plaintiff in BCCLA's Challenge to Medically Assisted Death Laws, Dies." News release, September 18, 2017. bccla.org/news/2017/09robyn-moro-plaintiff-bcclas-challenge-medically-assisted-death-laws-dies/.

Beaudoin, Gérald A. "Assisted Suicide in Canada: The Rodriguez Case (1993)." *Canadian Encyclopedia,* 2006, 2016. thecanadianencyclopedia.ca/en/article/rodriguez-case-1993/.

Blanken, Henk. "My Death Is Not My Own: The Limits of Legal Euthanasia." *The Guardian,* August 10, 2018. theguardian.com/news/2018/aug/10/my-death-is-not-my-own-the-limits-of-legal-euthanasia?CMP=Share_iosApp_Other.

Brean, Joseph. "Millennials Are More Likely to Believe in an Afterlife Than Are Older Generations." *National Post,* March 29, 2018. nationalpost.com/news/canada/millennials-do-you-believe-in-life-after-life.

British Broadcasting Corporation. "Who Was Alfie Evans and What Was the Row over His Treatment?" *BBC News*, April 28, 2018. bbc.com/news/uk-england-merseyside-43754949.

Canadian Broadcasting Corporation. "Woman Found Not Guilty in Assisted Suicide Case." *CBC News*, November 4, 2004. cbc.ca/news/canada/woman-found-not-guilty-in-assisted-suicide-case-1.515746.

Canadian Broadcasting Corporation. "'Compassionate Homicide': The Law and Robert Latimer." *CBC News*, December 6, 2010. cbc.ca/news/canada/compassionate-homicide-the-law-and-robert-latimer-1.972561.

Canadian Broadcasting Corporation. "Most Ontarians Would Prefer to Die at Home. Why Isn't That Happening?" *CBC News*, February 15, 2018. cbc.ca/news/canada/ottawa/dying-at-home-ontario-study-palliative-care-1.4534872.

Canadian Integrative Network for Death Education and Alternatives. "Introduction." cindea.ca.

Canadian Virtual Hospice. "Health Care Directives." December 2017. virtualhospice.ca/en_US/Main+Site+Navigation/Home/Topics/Topics/Decisions/Health+Care+Directives.aspx.

Chalkley-Rhoden, Stephanie. "Euthanasia Advocate Dr. Rodney Syme Wins Appeal Against Medical Board Ban." *Australian Broadcasting Corporation*, December 21, 2016. abc.net.au/news/2016-12-22/euthanasia-advocate-dr-rodney-syme-wins-medical-board-appeal/8142620.

Cook, Morven. "Assisted Suicide, The Musical: We Must Consider How the Debate Around Euthanasia Is Framed in the Arts." *The Independent*, November 22, 2016. independent.co.uk/arts-entertainment/theatre-dance/features/assisted-suicide-a-musical-a7431446.html.

Covenant Health. "Theological Reflection in Support of: Covenant Health's End-of-Life and Palliative Care Strategy." September 16, 2011. covenanthealth.ca/resources/AboutUs_TheologicalReflections_TheologicalReflectioninSupportofCovenant%20HealthsPalliativeandEndofLifeStrategy.pdf.

Death Café. "What Is Death Café?" deathcafe.com/what/.

Dignitas. "Countries With End-of-Life Help Laws and/or Regulations." dignitas.ch/index.php?option=com_content&view=article&id=54&Itemid=88&lang=en.

Dixon, Annabel. "I Took My Sister to Dignitas." *Metro News*, July 12, 2018. metro.co.uk/2018/07/12/i-took-my-sister-to-dignitas-7697964/?ito=article.desktop.share.top.twitter.

Downie, Joceylyn, and Jennifer Chandler. "Can We Die? The Seriously Ill Need Clarity." *The Conversation*, April 23, 2018. theconversation.com/can-we-die-the-seriously-ill-need-clarity-94475.

Dying With Dignity Canada. "Fair Access to Medical Assistance in Dying." dyingwithdignity.ca/fair_access.

Exit International. "Philip Nitschke." exitinternational.net/about-exit/dr-philip-nitschke/.

Farrell, Michael J. "As Assisted Suicide and Euthanasia Issues Simmer, Look at Holland." *National Catholic Reporter*, April 11, 1997. questia.com/read/1G1-19325538/as-assisted-suicide-and-euthanasia-issues-simmer.

Ferguson, Pamela R. "Causing Death or Allowing to Die? Developments in the Law." *Journal of Medical Ethics* 23 (1997). jme.bmj.com/content/medethics/23/6/368.full.pdf.

Hosford, Paul. "Gail O'Rorke Found Not Guilty of Assisting the Suicide of Her Friend." *TheJournal.ie*, April 28, 2015. thejournal.ie/assisted-suicide-a-crime-if-suicide-isnt-2073607-Apr2015/.

"Japan Society for Dying with Dignity." songenshi-kyokai.com/english.

Journeying Beyond. "Death Midwifery." beyonds.ca/Journeying/home.html.

Kaplan, Bette Weinstein. "Hospice versus Palliative Care: Understanding the Distinction." *Oncology Nurse Advisor*, May 1, 2010. oncologynurseadvisor.com/the-total-patient/ hospice-versus-palliative-care-understanding-the-distinction/article/168852/.

Keown, John. "Medical Murder by Omission? The Law and Ethics of Withholding and Withdrawing Treatment and Tube Feeding." *Clinical Medicine* 3, no. 5 (September/October 2003). www.clinmed.rcpjournal.org/content/3/5/460.full.pdf+html

Leiva, Rene. "When Suicide Becomes Banal." *CMAJ Blogs*, November 24, 2015. cmajblogs.com/ when-suicide-becomes-banal/.

Martindale, Diane. "A Culture of Death." *Scientific American*, June 1, 2005. scientificamerican.com/article/a-culture-of-death/.

Multiple Sclerosis Society of Canada. "MS Society Funded Researcher Explores Rates of Suicide in People with MS." June 20, 2017. mssociety.ca/research-news/article/ ms-society-funded-researcher-explores-rates-of-suicide-in-people-with-ms.

National Council on Aging. "Elder Abuse Facts." ncoa.org/public-policy-action/elder-justice/ elder-abuse-facts/.

"Nitschke's 'Suicide Machine' Draws Crowds at Amsterdam Funeral Fair." *The Guardian*, April 15, 2018. theguardian.com/society/2018/apr/15/nitschke-suicide- machine-amsterdam-euthanasia-funeral-fair.

Oregon Health Authority. "Death with Dignity Act." Oregon.gov/oha/ph/ProviderPartnerResources/ EvaluationResearch/DeathwithDignityAct/Pages/ors/aspx.

Porter, Catherine. "At His Own Wake, Celebrating Life and the Gift of Death." *New York Times*, May 25, 2017. nytimes.com/2017/05/25/world/canada/euthanasia-bill-john-shields-death.html.

Priest, Lisa. "How Much Does Dying Cost Canadians?" *Globe and Mail*, November 28, 2011/May 3, 2018. theglobeandmail.com/life/health-and-fitness/how-much-does-dying-cost-canadians/article554853/.

ProCon.org. "Do Euthanasia and Physician-Assisted Suicide Ensure a Good Death?" euthanasia.procon.org/view.answers.php?questionID=000190#answer-id-001267.

ProCon.org. "Do Euthanasia and Physician-Assisted Suicide Violate the Hippocratic Oath?" eutha- nasia.procon.org/view.answers.php?questionID=000198.

Psychology Today. "Bereavement." psychologytoday.com/ca/conditions/bereavement.

Public Health England. "Statistical Commentary: End of Life Care Profiles, February 2018 Update." Official Statistics, February 6, 2018. gov.uk/ government/publications/end-of-life-care-profiles-february-2018-update/ statistical-commentary-end-of-life-care-profiles-february-2018-update.

RAND Institute. "Planning for the Rising Costs of Dementia." rand.org/capabilities/solutions/plan- ning-for-the-rising-costs-of-dementia.html.

Schadenberg, Alex. "Netherlands' 2017 Euthanasia Deaths Increase by Another 8%." *National Right to Life News*, March 8, 2018. nationalrighttolifenews.org/news/2018/03/ netherlands-2017-euthanasia-deaths-increase-by-another-8/.

Sikkema, John. "No Need to Override the Charter to Pass a New Assisted Suicide Law." *National Post*, September 24, 2015. nationalpost.com/opinion/ john-sikkema-no-need-to-override-the-charter-to-pass-a-new-assisted-suicide-law.

Stolberg, Michael. "Two Pioneers of Euthanasia around 1800." *Hastings Center Report* 38, no. 3 (2008). questia.com/read/1G1-187426951/two-pioneers-of-euthanasia-around-1800.

Ubel, Peter A. "Assisted Suicide and the Case of Dr. Quill and Diane." *Issues in Law and Medicine* 8, no. 4 (1993). questia.com/read/1G1-13723276/assisted-suicide-and-the-case-of-dr-quill-and-diane.

Vallely, Paul. "Child Euthanasia: Too Hard to Live, Too Young to Die." *The Independent*, February 16, 2014. independent.co.uk/life-style/health-and-families/health-news/child-euthanasia-too-hard-to-live-too-young-to-die-9131089.html.

Vitelli, Romeo. "The Case of Timothy Quill." *Providentia* (blog), May 24, 2015. drvitelli.typepad.com/providentia/2015/05/the-case-of-timothy-quill.html.

Wade, Derek T., and Claire Johnston. "The Permanent Vegetative State: Practical Guidance on Diagnosis and Management." *British Medical Journal,* September 25, 1999. ncbi.nlm.nih.gov/pmc/articles/PMC1116668/.

Williams, Susan Schneider. "The Terrorist Inside My Husband's Brain." *Neurology*, September 26, 2016. n.neurology.org/content/87/13/1308.

World Federation of Right to Die Societies. "Questions and Answers." worldrtd.net/questions-and-answers.

Zamichow, Nora, and Ken Murray. "The Hippocratic Oath and the Terminally Ill." *Los Angeles Times*, December 26, 2014. latimes.com/opinion/op-ed/la-oe-zamichow-murray-hippocratic-oath-death-20141228-story.html.

Zitter, Jessica Nutik. "Should I Help My Patients Die?" *New York Times*, August 5, 2017. nytimes.com/2017/08/05/opinion/sunday/dying-doctors-palliative-medicine.html.

Zitter, Jessica Nutik. "What's Ignored in the Debate over Aid in Dying." *San Francisco Chronicle*, June 18, 2018. sfchronicle.com/opinion/openforum/article/What-s-ignored-in-the-debate-over-aid-in-dying-13004832.php

## Multimedia

Calderone, Andrew, and Troy Moth, dirs. *Exit Interview: John Hofsess.* Documentary film, 44:00. Literary Films, 2018.

Canadian Broadcasting Corporation. "Assisted Dying: What Happens When Doctors Disagree on What the Law Says?" Video, 9:48. *The National*, December 12, 2017. cbc.ca/player/play/1115250755920/.

Cohen, Janine, prod. "My Conscience Tells Me." Video, 30:45. Australian Broadcasting Corporation, March 7, 2016. abc.net.au/austory/my-conscience-tells-me/7225072.

Harris, Sam. "The Lessons of Death: A Conversation with Frank Ostaseski." Podcast, 1:07:59. *Waking Up*, episode 104, November 15, 2017. samharris.org/podcasts/the-lessons-of-death/.

Krauss, Dan, dir. *Extremis.* Documentary film, 24:00. Netflix, 2016.

Larry, Sheldon, dir. *At the End of the Day: The Sue Rodriguez Story.* TV movie, 1:29:00. Atlantic Mediaworks, 1998.

Thornton, John, prod. "My Life—My Choice: Dying With Dignity." Video, 45:00. M2TV for Vision TV, 2016. visiontv.ca/videos/my-life-my-choice/.

Wilson, Tim, dir. *Griefwalker.* Documentary film, 1:10.12. National Film Board of Canada, 2008. nfb.ca/film/griefwalker/.

# *Photo Credits*

p. iv: Helga Williams

**Introduction**: p. 4: Nikki Tate; p. 6: wjarek/Shutterstock.com; p. 8: FatCamera/istock.com

**Chapter One**: p. 12: *The Times Colonist*/Bruce Stotesbury; p. 13: Helga Williams; Courtesy of Nikki Tate; p. 15: Courtesy of Nikki Tate; p. 16: AP photo/Charles Dharapak; p. 17: Peter Marshall/Alamy Stock Photo

**Chapter Two**: p. 22: rubberball/fotosearch; p. 23: Wikimedia/Gordon Watts; p. 25: Jackie Cohen Photography; p. 29: Classic Image/Alamy Stock Photo; p. 31: Wavebreakmedia/Shutterstock.com

**Chapter Three**: p. 36: grandriver/iStock.com; p. 38: Derek Bayes (Courtesy of Angela Bayes); p. 40: Courtesy of Christopher Saunders

**Chapter Four**: p. 44: Augenstern/Shutterstock.com; p. 48: Letzte Olung, Dutch School c. 1600/Wikimedia Commons; p. 49: Wikipedia; p. 50: KatarzynaBialasiewicz/iStock; p. 55: AP photo/Elaine Thompson

**Chapter Five**: p. 58: icedmocha/Shutterstock.com; p. 61: The Canadian Press/Justin Tang; p. 62: Glenbow Archives NC-81-63; p. 66/67: Carmine Marinelli/Vancouver 24hrs/QMI; p. 69: Richard Sheinwald; p. 70: The Canadian Press/Ward Perrin; p. 71: Courtesy of Exit International; p. 73: Sonia Bonet/Shutterstock.com

**Chapter Six**: p. 76: Engraving by Peter Paul Rubens, courtesy of the National Library of Medicine/Wikipedia; p. 77: Welcomme Images/Wikipedia; p. 78: U.S. Food and Drug Administration/Wikimedia Commons; p. 79: Stipple engraving by H. Lehmann/Wellcome Collection; p. 81: Richard Ellis/Alamy Stock Photo; p. 82: *Daily Mail*/Shutterstock.com; p. 84: PA Images/Alamy Stock Photo; p. 87: Courtesy of Dying with Dignity Canada

**Chapter Seven**: p. 94: Viacheslav Lopatin/Shutterstock.com; p. 95: Jean-Michel Bigou, Canadian Religious Conference; p. 98: Radiokukka/iStock.com; p. 100: Troy Moth; p. 101: Courtesy of Dr. Richard Thain; p. 102: Fred Lum/*The Globe and Mail*; p. 103: Debra Brash/*The Times Colonist*

**Chapter Eight**: p. 107: John Dickey; p. 111: Gazet Van Antwerpen; p. 113: Eddie Pearson/Stocksy; p. 115: @Aurelia Brouwers/Instagram; p. 117: Vicki L. Miller/Shutterstock.com; p. 120: PictureLux/The Hollywood Archive/Alamy Stock Photo; p. 121: Courtesy of Sara Bennett Fox

**Chapter Nine**: p. 124: I AM NIKOM/Shutterstock.com; p. 126: The Canadian Press/Tom Hanson; p. 127: Shutterstock.com; p. 128: Nigel Bowles/Shutterstock.com; p. 129: TOP: London News Pictures/Shutterstock (top) SOPA Images Limited/Alamy Stock Photo (bottom); p. 131: Courtesy of Nikki Tate; p. 133: Courtesy of Nikki Tate

**Chapter Ten**: p. 136: Samuel Masinter; p. 140: Courtesy of the Library Archives and Special Collections, The College of Staten Island; p. 142: Bundesarchiv, Bild 183-2000-0110-500/CC-BY-SA 3.0; p. 147: Courtesy of Ellen Goodman; p. 149: beerblur/Shutterstock.com

**Chapter Eleven**: p. 152: Courtesy of Orphan Wisdom; p. 153: Brandy Gallagher; p. 154: Aisté Valiūté and Daumantas Plechavičius; p. 156: Todd Korol; p. 157: Leslye Davis/*The New York Times*/Redux; p. 158: Courtesy of Exit International; p. 160: Courtesy of Nikki Tate

# Index

Page numbers in **bold** indicate an image caption.